Modern R Programming Cookbook

Recipes to simplify your statistical applications

Jaynal Abedin

BIRMINGHAM - MUMBAI

Modern R Programming Cookbook

First published: October 2017

Production reference: 1051017

Published by Packt Publishing Ltd.
Livery Place
35 Livery Street
Birmingham
B3 2PB, UK.

ISBN 978-1-78712-905-4

www.packtpub.com

Credits

Author
Jaynal Abedin

Reviewer
Eilidh Troup

Commissioning Editor
Aaron Lazar

Acquisition Editor
Karan Sadawana

Content Development Editor
Zeeyan Pinheiro

Technical Editor
Vibhuti Gawde

Copy Editor
Karuna Narayanan

Project Coordinator
Vaidehi Sawant

Proofreader
Safis Editing

Indexer
Francy Puthiry

Graphics
Abhinash Sahu

Production Coordinator
Nilesh Mohite

About the Author

Jaynal Abedin is currently doing research as a PhD student at Unit for Biomedical Data Analytics (BDA) of INSIGHT at the National University of Ireland Galway. His research work is focused on the sports science and sports medicine area in a targeted project with ORRECO --an Irish startup company that provides evidence-based advice to individual athletes through biomarker and GPS data. Before joining INSIGHT as a PhD student he was leading a team of statisticians at an international public health research organization (icddr,b). His primary role there was to develop internal statistical capabilities for researchers who come from various disciplines. He was involved in designing and delivering statistical training to the researchers. He has a bachelors and masters degree in statistics, and he has written two books in R programming: *Data Manipulation with R* and *R Graphs Cookbook* (Second Edition) with Packt. His current research interests are predictive modeling to predict probable injury of an athlete and scoring extremeness of multivariate data to get an early signal of an anomaly. Moreover, he has an excellent reputation as a freelance R programmer and statistician in an online platform such as upwork.

About the Reviewer

Eilidh J. Troup is an applications consultant at EPCC in the University of Edinburgh. She is interested in making High Performance Computing accessible to new users, particularly to biologists. She works on a variety of software projects, including the Simple Parallel R INTerface (SPRINT).

www.PacktPub.com

For support files and downloads related to your book, please visit www.PacktPub.com.

Did you know that Packt offers eBook versions of every book published, with PDF and ePub files available? You can upgrade to the eBook version at www.PacktPub.com and as a print book customer, you are entitled to a discount on the eBook copy. Get in touch with us at service@packtpub.com for more details.

At www.PacktPub.com, you can also read a collection of free technical articles, sign up for a range of free newsletters and receive exclusive discounts and offers on Packt books and eBooks.

https://www.packtpub.com/mapt

Get the most in-demand software skills with Mapt. Mapt gives you full access to all Packt books and video courses, as well as industry-leading tools to help you plan your personal development and advance your career.

Why subscribe?

- Fully searchable across every book published by Packt
- Copy and paste, print, and bookmark content
- On demand and accessible via a web browser

Customer Feedback

Thanks for purchasing this Packt book. At Packt, quality is at the heart of our editorial process. To help us improve, please leave us an honest review on this book's Amazon page at https://www.amazon.com/dp/1787129055.

If you'd like to join our team of regular reviewers, you can e-mail us at customerreviews@packtpub.com. We award our regular reviewers with free eBooks and videos in exchange for their valuable feedback. Help us be relentless in improving our products!

Table of Contents

Preface

R is a high-level statistical language and is widely used among statisticians and data miners for developing statistical applications. The objective of this book is to show the readers how to work with different programming aspects of R. Emerging R developers and data scientists may have very good programming knowledge but their understanding of the R syntax and semantics could be limited. This book will be a platform to develop practical solutions to real-world problems in a scalable fashion and with very good understanding of R. You will work with various versions of R libraries that are essential for scalable data science solutions. You will learn to work with I/O issues when working with the relatively larger datasets. By the end of this book, you will also learn how to work with databases from within R.

What this book covers

Chapter 1, *Installing and Configuring R and its Libraries*, covers the recipes on how to install and configure R and its libraries on Windows and Linux platforms.

Chapter 2, *Data Structures in R*, covers the data structures of R and how to create and access their properties and various operations related to a specific data structure.

Chapter 3, *Writing Customized Functions*, guides you to create your own customized functions and understand how to work with various data types within a function and access an output of a function.

Chapter 4, *Conditional and Iterative Operations*, covers the use of conditional and repetition operators in R.

Chapter 5, *R Objects and Classes*, guides you in creating the S3 and S4 objects and how to use them in a variety of applications.

Chapter 6, *Querying, Filtering, and Summarizing*, introduces you to the dplyr library for data processing. This is one of the most popular libraries in R for data processing.

Chapter 7, *R for Text Processing*, covers the recipes related to working with unstructured text data.

Chapter 8, *R and Databases*, helps you learn how to interact with a database management system to develop statistical applications.

Chapter 9, *Parallel Processing in R*, uses the parallel processing approach to solve memory problems with a larger datasetand uses the XDF file for processing.

What you need for this book

This book requires the following to be set up:
• Base R
• RStudio IDE
• Microsoft R Client
• R tools for Visual Studio
• PostgreSQL database server

Who this book is for

This book is for developers who would like to enhance their R programming skills. Some basic knowledge of R programming is assumed.

Sections

In this book, you will find several headings that appear frequently (Getting ready, How to do it..., How it works..., There's more..., and See also). To give clear instructions on how to complete a recipe, we use these sections as follows:

Getting ready

This section tells you what to expect in the recipe, and describes how to set up any software or any preliminary settings required for the recipe.

How to do it...

This section contains the steps required to follow the recipe.

How it works...

This section usually consists of a detailed explanation of what happened in the previous section.

There's more...

This section consists of additional information about the recipe in order to make the reader more knowledgeable about the recipe.

See also

This section provides helpful links to other useful information for the recipe.

Conventions

In this book, you will find a number of text styles that distinguish between different kinds of information. Here are some examples of these styles and an explanation of their meaning. Code words in text, database table names, folder names, filenames, file extensions, pathnames, dummy URLs, user input, and Twitter handles are shown as follows: "Execute the following code to create numeric and logical vectors using the `c()` function" A block of code is set as follows:

```
cVec <- c("Cricket", "Football", "Basketball", "Rugby")
```

Any command-line input or output is written as follows:

```
lsb_release -a
```

New terms and **important words** are shown in bold. Words that you see on the screen, for example, in menus or dialog boxes, appear in the text like this: "On this web page, you will see **base** under the **Subdirectories** category."

Warnings or important notes appear like this.

Tips and tricks appear like this.

Reader feedback

Feedback from our readers is always welcome. Let us know what you think about this book-what you liked or disliked. Reader feedback is important to us as it helps us develop titles that you will really get the most out of. To send us general feedback, simply email feedback@packtpub.com, and mention the book's title in the subject of your message. If there is a topic that you have expertise in and you are interested in either writing or contributing to a book, see our author guide at www.packtpub.com/authors.

Customer support

Now that you are the proud owner of a Packt book, we have a number of things to help you to get the most from your purchase.

Downloading the example code

You can download the example code files for this book from your account at http://www.packtpub.com. If you purchased this book elsewhere, you can visit http://www.packtpub.com/support and register to have the files emailed directly to you. You can download the code files by following these steps:

1. Log in or register to our website using your email address and password.
2. Hover the mouse pointer on the **SUPPORT** tab at the top.
3. Click on **Code Downloads & Errata**.
4. Enter the name of the book in the **Search** box.
5. Select the book for which you're looking to download the code files.
6. Choose from the drop-down menu where you purchased this book from.
7. Click on **Code Download**.

You can also download the code files by clicking on the **Code Files** button on the book's web page at the Packt Publishing website. This page can be accessed by entering the book's name in the **Search** box. Please note that you need to be logged in to your Packt account. Once the file is downloaded, please make sure that you unzip or extract the folder using the latest version of:

- WinRAR / 7-Zip for Windows
- Zipeg / iZip / UnRarX for Mac
- 7-Zip / PeaZip for Linux

The code bundle for the book is also hosted on GitHub at `https://github.com/PacktPublishing/Modern-R-Programming-Cookbook/`. We also have other code bundles from our rich catalog of books and videos available at `https://github.com/PacktPublishing/`. Check them out!

Errata

Although we have taken every care to ensure the accuracy of our content, mistakes do happen. If you find a mistake in one of our books-maybe a mistake in the text or the code-we would be grateful if you could report this to us. By doing so, you can save other readers from frustration and help us improve subsequent versions of this book. If you find any errata, please report them by visiting `http://www.packtpub.com/submit-errata`, selecting your book, clicking on the **Errata Submission Form** link, and entering the details of your errata. Once your errata are verified, your submission will be accepted and the errata will be uploaded to our website or added to any list of existing errata under the Errata section of that title. To view the previously submitted errata, go to `https://www.packtpub.com/books/content/support` and enter the name of the book in the search field. The required information will appear under the **Errata** section.

Piracy

Piracy of copyrighted material on the internet is an ongoing problem across all media. At Packt, we take the protection of our copyright and licenses very seriously. If you come across any illegal copies of our works in any form on the internet, please provide us with the location address or website name immediately so that we can pursue a remedy. Please contact us at `copyright@packtpub.com` with a link to the suspected pirated material. We appreciate your help in protecting our authors and our ability to bring you valuable content.

Questions

If you have a problem with any aspect of this book, you can contact us at `questions@packtpub.com`, and we will do our best to address the problem.

1
Installing and Configuring R and its Libraries

In this chapter, you will be exposed to the recipes on how to install and configure R and its libraries in Windows and Linux platforms. Specifically, you will come across the following recipes:

- Installing and configuring base R in Windows
- Installing and configuring base R in Linux
- Installing and configuring RStudio IDE in Windows
- Installing and configuring RStudio IDE in Linux
- Installing and configuring R tools for Visual Studio in Windows
- Installing R libraries from various sources
- Installing a specific version of R library

Introduction

It is expected that you have basic knowledge of installing software on the platform that you use regularly. However, it is helpful to have an overview of some technical aspects of installing R and the **integrated development environment** (**IDE**) such as RStudio. This chapter will serve as a reference point for the technical issues during installation and configuration of R and its libraries for Windows and Linux platforms. Each of the recipes contains detailed description with the necessary screenshots so that you feel very comfortable, even if you are not in front of your computer. After completing all the recipes of this chapter, you will be confident enough to install R and its libraries in Windows and Linux platforms. So, let's get started.

Installing and configuring base R in Windows

In this recipe, you will learn to install R in the Windows platform and we will address other necessary configuration issues that are related to the Windows operating system.

Getting ready

To start this recipe, you will need to know your version of the Windows operating system, for example, whether it is Windows 7, 8, or 10. Also, you need to know specific architecture, such as 32-bit or 64-bit. Once you know the particulars of the operating system, you are ready to install base R by following the steps in the next section. Another thing that you need to check is whether R is already installed on your computer or not. You can easily check by inspecting the **Start** menu or task bar or desktop icon. Now, let's assume that you did not install R previously in your computer and this is the first time you are going to do so.

Once you get detailed information about your operating system, you will need to download the executable file for the Windows operating system. To find the latest version of R, you can visit the **Comprehensive R Archive Network (CRAN)** at `http://cran.r-project.org/`. On this web page, you will get to know the latest release of R and other related information.

To download the latest release of R for Windows, perform the following steps:

1. Visit `https://cran.r-project.org/bin/windows/`, which will show you the following screen:

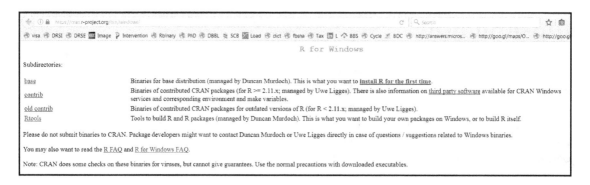

2. On this web page, you will see **base** under the **Subdirectories** category. As a first-time user of R, you need to download the executable file from this link.

3. Once you click on **base**, you will end up on this page, `https://cran.r-project.org/bin/windows/base/` as shown in the following screenshot:

4. Now, click on **Download R 3.x.x (This version number might differ because during preparation of this recipe, the version was 3.3.3) for Windows**. The executable file will be downloaded into your local storage.

How to do it...

Once you have downloaded the executable file, you are ready to install it on your computer. Perform the following steps and choose the options accordingly. The screenshots are for your convenience only:

1. Go to the folder where you have stored the executable file that you have downloaded, by following the instructions in the previous section.

You must have administrator privileges to install the software.

2. If you have administrator privileges, then just double-click on the executable file, or right-click on the mouse and select **Run as administrator**:

3. In Windows 7, it will show a notification with the title **User Access Control**. In this case, you must choose **Yes** to proceed.

4. The first thing it will ask you to do is choose a language, as shown in the following screenshot. Once you select your chosen language, click on the **OK** button. The R Setup Wizard will appear, and you will see various options to select in different pages:

5. Click on **Next >** on this page to proceed with the installation:

6. On this page, the **GNU GENERAL PUBLIC LICENSE** information will be displayed, and you will be asked to read and understand the licensing agreement and then click on the **Next >** button:

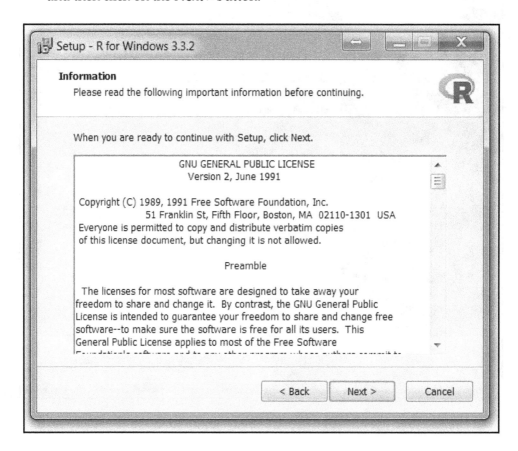

7. Now, you will be asked to choose the destination folder where you want to store the installation files. Usually, by default, it shows `C:/Program Files/`, and sometimes, it also shows one more level `C:/Program Files/R/R-x.x.x`. You can keep the default location, or you can choose a separate destination based on your choice. Once you have selected the destination, click on the **Next >** button:

8. At this stage, you will get the option to select the component that you want to install. You can choose either **32-bit Files** only, **64-bit Files** only, or both along with core files and message translation. After selecting the components, again click on the **Next >** button:

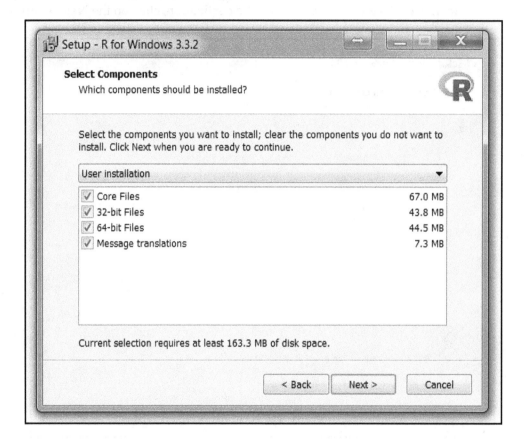

9. Now, you will be asked whether you want to customize your startup or accept the defaults. The recommended option at this stage is to accept the defaults and click on the **Next >** button:

10. You can decide whether you want to create the start menu folder or not and you can specify its name at this stage of installation:

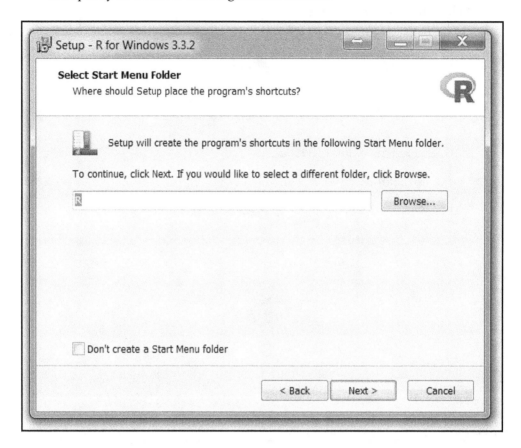

11. Finally, you will be given the option to choose whether you want to create a desktop icon and also create a quick launch icon. You can specify whether you want to save the version number into the computer's registry or not, and the last option is to associate file name extensions .R and .RData with the software. Once you are done with selecting the options, click on **Next >** and the installation will be started:

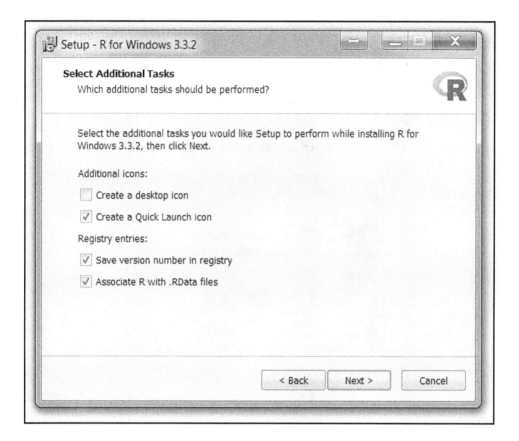

How it works...

Once you follow the steps described in the *How to do it...* section, the R software will be installed, and it's ready to use. You can open R using either the desktop icon or quick launch icon, or from the **Start** menu.

However, to do some advanced-level work in R or if you want to open the R console from the Windows Command Prompt, you need to do some configuration that is specific to the operating system. In this subsection, you will see how the configuration works.

If you want to access the R terminal from the Windows Command Prompt, then you must open the Windows Command Prompt, and then type R and press *Enter*. However, without correctly configuring R, you won't be able to open the R terminal in this way. The following are the steps to configure R:

1. Right-click on the **Computer** icon and select **Properties** from the following screen:

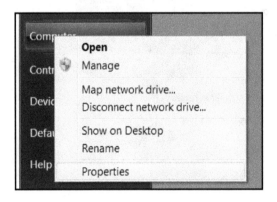

2. Now, click on **Advanced system settings**. It will open up the **System Properties** window as shown in the following screenshot:

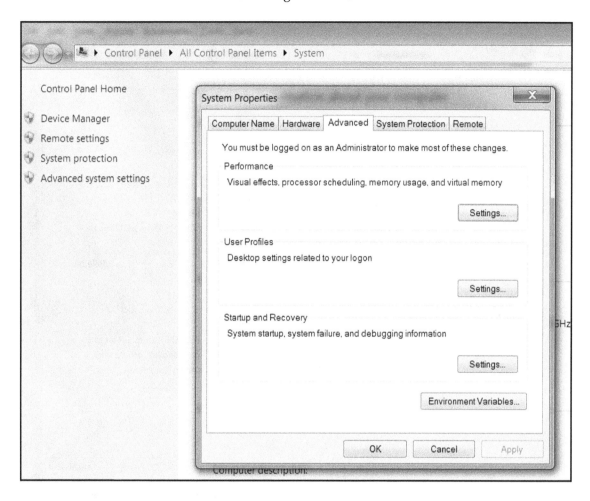

3. At the bottom of the **System Properties** window, you will see **Environment Variables....** Click on it and it will show the following screen:

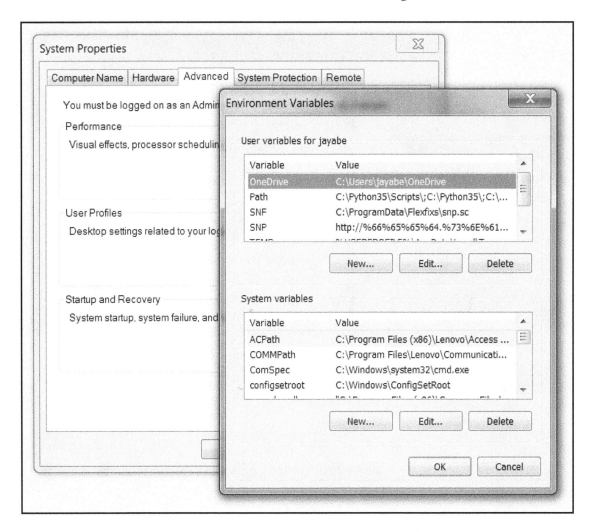

4. The **Environment Variables** window will pop up in which you will see two separate sections, one for **User variables** and another for **System variables**.

5. In the **System variables** section, select the **Path** variable and then click on **Edit...**:

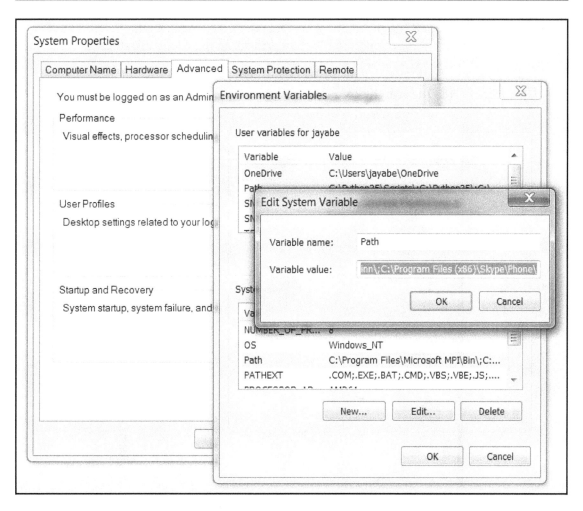

6. Now, in this **Path** variable, add the location where you have installed R software. Choose the location where the `R.exe and R.dll` file belongs, for example, `C:\Program Files\R\R-3.3.2\bin\x64`.

7. Put the location at the end of the **Path** variable after putting in a semicolon (`;`) and then click on **OK** on each of the window opened.

Once you have performed the preceding steps, it is the time to check whether you have correctly configured environment variables by performing the following steps:

1. Go to the **Start** menu.
2. Type cmd in the search box.
3. Then, click on **cmd.exe**. It will open a black screen called Windows Command Prompt:

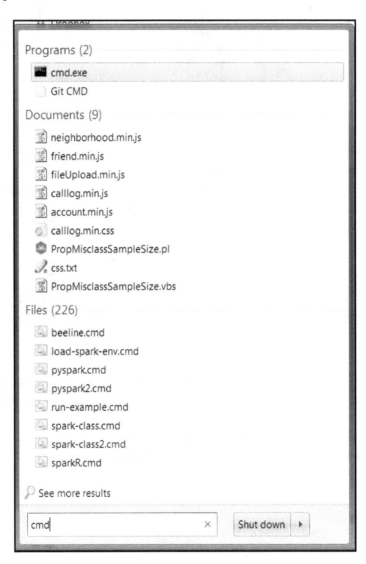

4. Type R and hit *Enter*. If the R console opens, then everything is alright and you have correctly configured R in Windows:

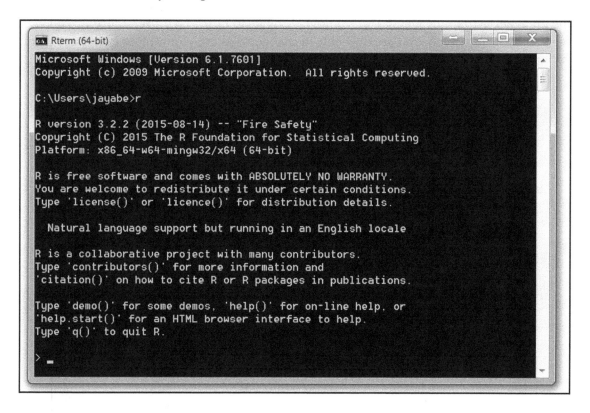

There's more...

If you want to customize the R console, its display font, font size, and others, you can edit the preferences from the menu. For example, navigate to **Edit | GUI preference...**. You will see the following screen. You are now able to change anything you want to customize your R console and other things:

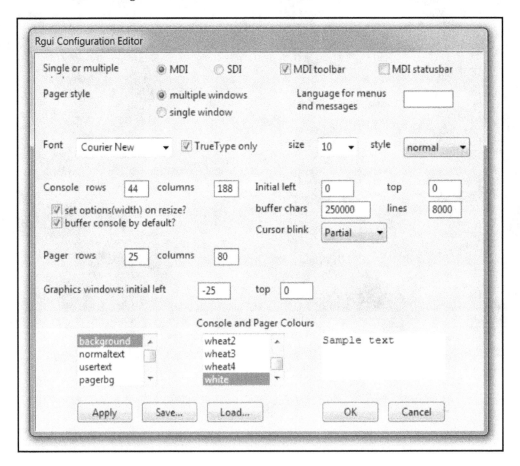

See also

In this recipe, you have gone through the steps based on the Windows operating system. If you want to install and configure R for Linux, see the next recipe *Installing and configuring base R in Linux*.

Installing and configuring base R in Linux

It is not necessarily the case that every user will use Windows platform. In this recipe, you will see how to install and configure R on the Linux platform. Each of the steps is described with an appropriate screenshot so that you can easily understand the steps.

Getting ready

To install R in the Linux operating system, first, you need to know the version of Linux you are using. To know the version of Linux installed on your computer, there are many options. One of the options is the following command:

```
lsb_release -a
```

This command will give the release information as shown in the following screenshot:

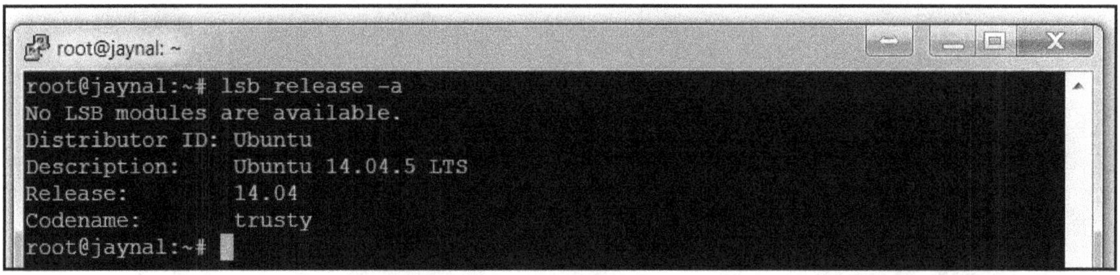

In this recipe, you will see the example from the Ubuntu 14.04 release.

How to do it...

Once you have the version number, you simply need to install base R onto your computer. The step-by-step procedure is as follows:

1. Update `etc/apt/source.list` by adding an entry as follows:

   ```
   deb <cran mirror address>/bin/linux/ubuntu trusty/
   ```

2. Replace `<cran mirror address>` by putting an actual mirror link from the list of available mirrors from `https://cran.r-project.org/mirrors.html`. Remember that you must have administrator privileges to edit `etc/apt/source.list`.

3. Once you have performed the preceding step, type the following command to install R:

```
sudo apt-get update
sudo apt-get install r-base
```

4. The preceding two commands will complete the installation process and you can check whether R has been installed correctly or not, by typing R and hitting *Enter* on the Terminal window. If the R console opens, then you are ready to go:

```
root@jaynal:~# R

R version 3.3.2 (2016-10-31) -- "Sincere Pumpkin Patch"
Copyright (C) 2016 The R Foundation for Statistical Computing
Platform: x86_64-pc-linux-gnu (64-bit)

R is free software and comes with ABSOLUTELY NO WARRANTY.
You are welcome to redistribute it under certain conditions.
Type 'license()' or 'licence()' for distribution details.

  Natural language support but running in an English locale

R is a collaborative project with many contributors.
Type 'contributors()' for more information and
'citation()' on how to cite R or R packages in publications.

Type 'demo()' for some demos, 'help()' for on-line help, or
'help.start()' for an HTML browser interface to help.
Type 'q()' to quit R.

>
```

5. Some of the users may need to compile R packages from the source code. In that case, you will need to install the following component of R:

```
sudo apt-get install r-base-dev
```

 Your computer must connect to the internet to install R.

There's more...

In this recipe, you have installed base R into Ubuntu 14.04 release. If your operating system has another release of Linux, then visit `https://cran.r-project.org/`, select **Download R for Linux**, and follow the steps outlined there.

See also

To understand how to install an IDE into either Windows or Linux, follow the next recipe.

Installing and configuring RStudio IDE in Windows

In the first two recipes, the steps were related to installing base R. To use R with an IDE where syntax highlighting features are available along with other options, you will need to install a preferred IDE software. RStudio is one of the most popular IDEs for R. In this recipe, you will learn from where, and how, to download RStudio and install it onto your computer.

Getting ready

To install an IDE, the first step is to install base R; that is, **you need to make sure R has been installed prior to installing RStudio IDE**. RStudio is an open source and enterprise-ready professional software for R. Now, let's take a look at the following few steps to download and install RStudio IDE:

1. To download open source components of RStudio IDE, visit the web page at `https://www.rstudio.com/products/rstudio/`.

2. From this link, choose RStudio for desktop and download the executable file. The latest version of RStudio is 1.0.136 at the time of the preparation of this recipe. Select an appropriate executable file from the list that matches with your operating system:

RStudio Desktop 1.0.136 — Release Notes

RStudio requires R 2.11.1+. If you don't already have R, download it here.

Installers for Supported Platforms

Installers	Size	Date	MD5
RStudio 1.0.136 - Windows Vista/7/8/10	81.9 MB	2016-12-21	93b3f307f567c33f7a4db4c114099b3e
RStudio 1.0.136 - Mac OS X 10.6+ (64-bit)	71.2 MB	2016-12-21	12d6d6ade0203a2fcef6fe3dea65c1ae
RStudio 1.0.136 - Ubuntu 12.04+/Debian 8+ (32-bit)	85.5 MB	2016-12-21	0a20fb89d8aaeb39b329a640ddadd2c5
RStudio 1.0.136 - Ubuntu 12.04+/Debian 8+ (64-bit)	92.1 MB	2016-12-21	2a73b88a12a9fbaf96251cecf8b41340
RStudio 1.0.136 - Fedora 19+/RedHat 7+/openSUSE 13.1+ (32-bit)	84.7 MB	2016-12-21	fa6179a7855bff0f939a34c169da45fd
RStudio 1.0.136 - Fedora 19+/RedHat 7+/openSUSE 13.1+ (64-bit)	85.7 MB	2016-12-21	2b3a148ded380b704e58496befb55545

How to do it...

The following steps will help you go through the installation process:

1. Go to the folder where you have stored the executable file of the latest release of RStudio:

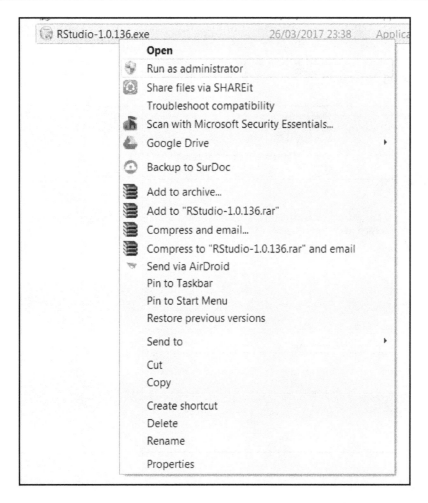

2. Right-click on it and select **Run as administrator**. The installation Wizard will open. Then, click on **Next >** on this screen.

3. At this stage, you will be asked to give the location where you want to install it. The default location usually shows as `C:\Program Files\RStudio`. However, if you want to install into a different location, then you can do this from here and click on **Next >**:

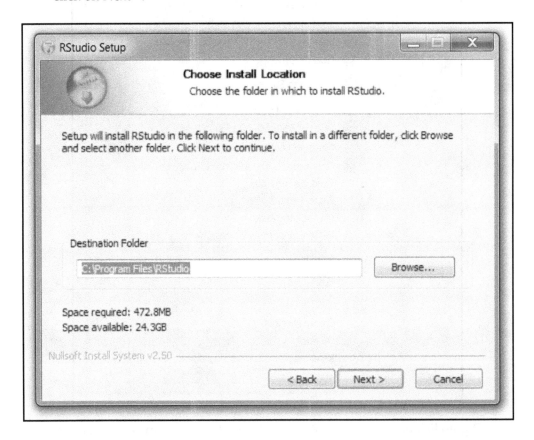

4. Now, you will be asked to give a name of the start menu folder and then click on **Install**.

How it works...

Once you run the executable file of RStudio, it then checks whether there is any base R installed in the computer. If you do not already have R installed, then you will be given a message stating that base R is required to install RStudio. Once you have made sure that base R is already installed, it will install the IDE without any errors by following the steps mentioned in the *How to do it...* section.

There's more...

The following screenshot is the initial user interface of RStudio where you will see four major components:

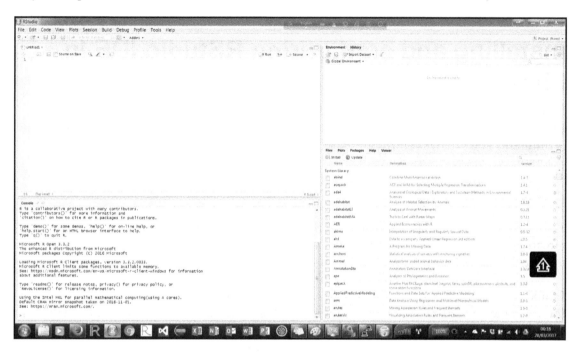

Let's take a look at the following four major components shown in the preceding screenshot:

- In the upper-left section is the R script writing section where you will usually write R code to solve your data analytics, data management, or data visualization problems.
- In the lower-left section is the R console where you will be able to see immediate output and error messages along the line of code that has been run already.
- The upper-right section contains the history of R sessions and the current global environment. The environment section displays all current active R objects, their type, and other information.
- The lower-right corner contains several subcomponents, for example, the **Help** documentation window, graphical output (the **Plots** tab), the **Files** tab showing the list of files and folders in the selected directory, and also the list of R packages (the **Packages** tab).

See also

There is another similar IDE available, R tools for Visual Studio. This is another IDE developed and released by Microsoft. You will come into this recipe in this chapter.

Installing and configuring RStudio IDE in Linux

In this recipe, you will see how to install RStudio IDE in the Linux operating system. The RStudio IDE user interface will be the same as that in Windows, but the installation process is different. You will walk through the process with the appropriate screenshot.

Getting ready

To install RStudio IDE, the prior requirement is to install base R. Let's assume that base R is already installed on the computer. Now, visit the following web page and download the appropriate installer from the available list at `https://www.rstudio.com/products/rstudio/` and store it in the home directory for convenience. Depending on the version of Linux, the executable file comes with the various formats. In this recipe, you will download the `.deb` file and store it in the home directory. Also, you can directly install it from the internet using the `wget` command with the appropriate link to the file such as `https://download1.rstudio.org/rstudio-1.0.136-amd64.deb`.

How to do it...

Once you have downloaded the appropriate executable file, you are ready to install it. Since, you have downloaded the `.deb` file, you will require `gdebi-core` to execute that file. Here are the steps to install `gdebi-core` and then install RStudio IDE:

1. To install `gdebi-core`, run the following command:

   ```
   sudo apt-get install gdebi-core
   ```

2. To download the RStudio IDE installer `.deb` file, run the following command:

   ```
   wget https://download1.rstudio.org/rstudio-1.0.136-amd64.deb
   ```

The preceding command would generate the following output:

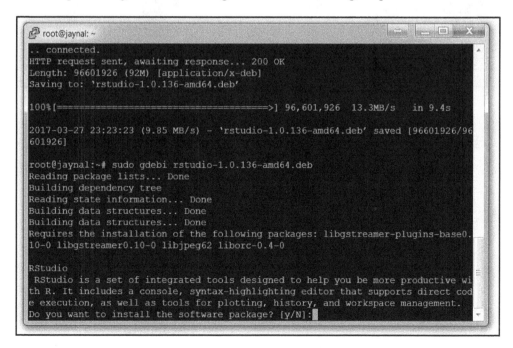

3. To install the IDE, run the following command:

```
sudo gdebi rstudio-1.0.136-amd64.deb
```

The preceding command will generate the following output:

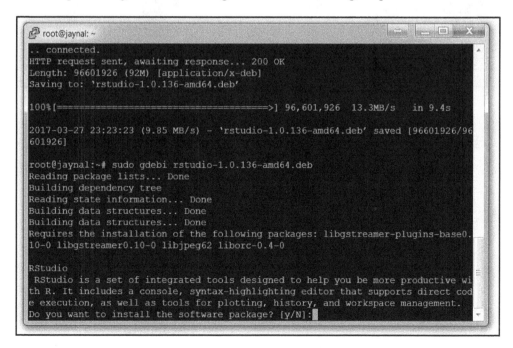

4. In the preceding screenshot, the terminal is asking whether you want to install the software or not. Type y and hit the *Enter* button here. Once the installation process is completed, you will see the following screen in the Terminal:

```
root@jaynal: ~
Unpacking libgstreamer0.10-0:amd64 (0.10.36-1.2ubuntu3) ...
Selecting previously unselected package liborc-0.4-0:amd64.
Preparing to unpack .../liborc-0.4-0_1%3a0.4.18-1ubuntu1_amd64.deb ...
Unpacking liborc-0.4-0:amd64 (1:0.4.18-1ubuntu1) ...
Selecting previously unselected package libgstreamer-plugins-base0.10-0:amd64.
Preparing to unpack .../libgstreamer-plugins-base0.10-0_0.10.36-1.1ubuntu2_amd64
.deb ...
Unpacking libgstreamer-plugins-base0.10-0:amd64 (0.10.36-1.1ubuntu2) ...
Selecting previously unselected package libjpeg62:amd64.
Preparing to unpack .../libjpeg62_6b1-4ubuntu1_amd64.deb ...
Unpacking libjpeg62:amd64 (6b1-4ubuntu1) ...
Setting up libgstreamer0.10-0:amd64 (0.10.36-1.2ubuntu3) ...
Setting up liborc-0.4-0:amd64 (1:0.4.18-1ubuntu1) ...
Setting up libgstreamer-plugins-base0.10-0:amd64 (0.10.36-1.1ubuntu2) ...
Setting up libjpeg62:amd64 (6b1-4ubuntu1) ...
Processing triggers for libc-bin (2.19-0ubuntu6.9) ...
Selecting previously unselected package rstudio.
(Reading database ... 82136 files and directories currently installed.)
Preparing to unpack rstudio-1.0.136-amd64.deb ...
Unpacking rstudio (1.0.136) ...
Setting up rstudio (1.0.136) ...
Processing triggers for shared-mime-info (1.2-0ubuntu3) ...
Processing triggers for mime-support (3.54ubuntu1.1) ...
root@jaynal:~#
```

 During installation, make sure you are connected to the internet.

How it works...

First, the `sudo apt-get install gdebi-core` command helps you download and install the `gdebi-core` package into the Linux system. By using the `wget` command, you are actually downloading the necessary file to install RStudio from the RStudio website. After that when you enter the `sudo gdebi rstudio-1.0.136-amd64.deb` command, it installs the software for you, and after completing this step, you are ready to use it.

See also

To know more about RStudio, you can visit the RStudio website for more documentation, but this recipe covered the most basic steps to install the software.

Installing and configuring R tools for Visual Studio in Windows

R Tools for Visual Studio (**RTVS**) is another development environment for R like RStudio, but it has extended facilities developed by Microsoft. RTVS is an extension of Visual Studio 2015, and it's free with the Community Edition of Visual Studio 2015. In this recipe, you will go through the installation process.

Getting ready

To install RTVS, your computer needs to fulfill some of the following prerequisites:

- Visual Studio 2015 Community Edition (this is freely available)
- Visual Studio Update 3 to install RTVS
- Microsoft R Open/Open source base R 64-bit with 3.2.1 or higher
- Microsoft R Client

How to do it...

Let's take a look at the following steps:

1. Download and install Visual Studio 2015 Community Edition and install Update 3 or install Visual Studio Community 2017.
2. Install Microsoft R Open or CRAN R 64-bit with R version 3.2.1 or higher.
3. Download and install R Client from `https://msdn.microsoft.com/en-us/microsoft-r/r-client-get-started`:

System Requirements:

Operating Systems:	64-bit versions of **Microsoft Windows 7, 8.1, and 10**
Free disk space:	600+ MB recommended, after installation of all prerequisites
Available RAM:	4+ GB recommended
Internet access:	Needed to download R Client and any dependencies

You must install Microsoft R Client to a local drive on your computer.

You may need to disable your antivirus software. If you do, please turn it back on as soon as you are finished.

4. Once you have completed the prerequisites, download and install RTVS from `https://aka.ms/rtvs-current`:

How it works...

Once the installation is completed, the user interface is similar to RStudio. Here is the screenshot of RTVS:

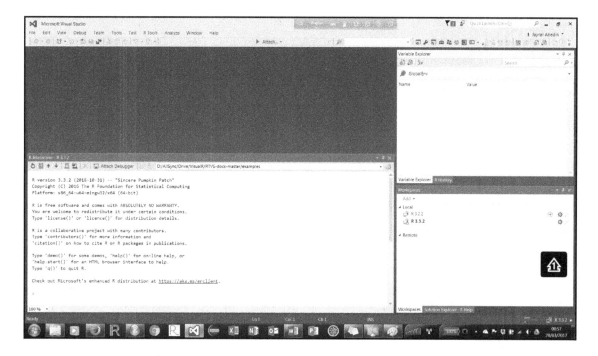

See also

Here are the relevant links for more information about RTVS. It is suggested that you take a look at them for updated information:

- https://www.visualstudio.com/vs/rtvs/
- https://docs.microsoft.com/en-us/visualstudio/rtvs/installation

Installing R libraries from various sources

R library or packages refer to a collection of previously programmed functions for specific tasks. When you install base R, you will see that it comes with a number of default libraries installed, but users need to use customized libraries to solve their problems. In this recipe, you will see how you can install libraries from different sources, such as CRAN, GitHub, and **Bioconductor** (**BioC**).

Getting ready

Suppose you are interested in visualizing your data using the ggplot2 library, but when you call the library using the library(ggplot2) code, you end up getting an error saying that ggplot2 is not found. Now, you need to install ggplot2. In this recipe, you will install the following libraries from the sources mentioned:

- The ggplot2 library from CRAN
- The devtools library from CRAN
- The dplyr library from GitHub
- The GenomicFeatures library from BioC

How to do it...

Under the default utils library, there is a function called install.packages() to install a package from within the R console. You can use the command install.packages(). This command will prompt you to select the appropriate server CRAN.

 To install packages using this approach, the computer must have an active internet connection.

The ggplot2 library

Lets take a look at the following steps to install the ggplot2 library:

1. Open the R console or terminal and then type the following command:

```
install.packages("ggplot2")
```

   The preceding command line will then ask you to select a server as follows:

```
install.packages("ggplot2")
--- Please select a CRAN mirror for use in this session ---
```

2. It will now install ggplot2 and its dependent libraries. If you want to avoid selecting a mirror server, then you can specify the mirror server within the install.packages() function using repos=.

The devtools library

This is another library that extends the functionalities of the `utils` library of base R. This library is convenient for developing various tools within R, and using this library, you can install the required library from GitHub. To install `devtools` along with its dependent libraries, use the `install.packages()` function as you did for `ggplot2`.

Installing a library from GitHub

To install any library from GitHub, you can use the `install_github()` function from the `devtools` library. You just need to know the name of the library and the GitHub ID of the repository owner. See the following installation code for the `dplyr` library from GitHub:

```
library(devtools)
install_github("hadley/dplyr")
```

Installing a library from the BioC repository

To install any library from the BioC repository, you have to use the `biocLite.R` file and then use the `biocLite()` function to install the library. The following code snippet is to install the `GenomicFeatures` library from the BioC repository:

```
source(https://bioconductor.org/biocLite.R)
biocLite("GenomicFeatures")
```

How it works...

In any of the commands to install a library, either `install.packages()`, `install_github()`, or `biocLite()`, first, it connects with the mirror server where the source code / binary-released version of the specified library is located. Then, it checks whether the dependent libraries are installed onto the computer or not. If the required dependent library is absent, then it will download and install those required libraries before installing the one you specified through the command. The command will also search for the location where the installed library will be stored. You can explicitly specify the location or you can use the default. The recommended approach is to specify a location and install all customized libraries into that folder.

To specify the installation location, you can use the `lib=` option within the function. Make sure you have created the folder that you are going to use as the destination folder. Here is an example:

```
install.packages("ggplot2", lib="c:/rPackages")
```

There's more...

Using `devtools`, you can install from either CRAN or from GitHub or even from the BioC repository. There are specific functions available within the `devtools` library as follows:

- `install_github()`
- `install_bioc()`
- `install_bitbucket()`
- `install_cran()`
- `install_git()`

See also

The user might need a specific version of a library to do a certain task, and that version could be an older one. To install the specific version of the library, see the next recipe that talks about it.

Installing a specific version of R library

Open source software is being updated by the maintainers and new features are being added to the existing ones. Sometimes, a task is dependent on a specific version of a library. In this recipe, you will see how to install a specific version of a library and how to check the version of an installed library.

Getting ready

To install a specific version of an R library, there is another facility available. The necessary functions are bound into the `versions` library to do this job. You need to install `versions` before using the function within it. To get ready, you have to run the following command:

```
install.packages("versions")
```

How to do it...

Take a look at the following steps:

1. If you want to check which version of ggplot2 has been installed onto your computer, you can run the following command:

    ```
    library(versions)
    installed.versions("ggplot2")
    ```

    The preceding command will show the following output on the console screen:

    ```
    > installed.versions("ggplot2")
    Checking package in 'C:/rPackages'
    (as 'lib' is unspecified)
    [1] "2.2.0"
    >
    ```

2. Now, to install the required version of any library, you first need to know the version number and how that has been written in the library documentation. Then, use that version number as follows:

    ```
    install.versions("ggplot2", versions = "2.2.0")
    ```

How it works...

Whenever you call the installed.versions() function, it looks at the DESCRIPTION file of that library and extracts the version number and displays it on the console.

Alternatively, whenever you call install.versions() to install the specified version of a library, it checks the date of that version and runs the install.dates() function internally to download the appropriate version onto the computer.

2
Data Structures in R

In this chapter, you will learn about the data structures of R and how to create and access its properties, and various operations related to a specific data structure. The following recipes will be covered in this chapter:

- Creating a vector and accessing its properties
- Creating a matrix and accessing its properties
- Creating a data frame and accessing its properties
- Creating an array and accessing its properties
- Creating a list from a combination of vector, matrix, and data frames
- Converting a matrix to a data frame and a data frame to a matrix

Introduction

To use R most efficiently and effectively, you must understand the data types and data structures of R, because the Machine Learning algorithms such as **Support Vector Machine(SVM)**, decision tree, and even linear regression and logistic regression have optimization components. The use of the correct data types is the key part of the performance of optimization. Also, to perform matrix operations, the user must use matrix data types. Moreover, the user needs to know the use of correct variables into the statistical model, and understanding R data types is the important aspect in this area. Here are the data types that will help you store and manage your data correctly and efficiently:

- Character
- Numeric
- Logical

- Integer
- Complex

The data structure of R is the way to organize the dataset for data storage and analytics purposes. Each of the different data structures can contain certain types of data. The following are the most popular and primary structures in R:

- **Vector:** This can contain only one type of data
- **Matrix:** This contains only one type of data but in two-dimensional representation
- **Array:** This contains only one type of data and it can store data with more than two dimensional structure
- **Data frame**: This can contain mixed types of data, and it is also a two-dimensional representation
- **List:** This can contain heterogeneous data, including vector, matrix, data frames, and even the list itself

By going through each of the recipes in this chapter, you will learn to create, modify, and access the properties, and perform certain operations on various types of data.

Creating a vector and accessing its properties

In this recipe, you will learn what a vector is in R, and how to create it, access its properties, and perform certain operations.

Getting ready

To follow this recipe, you need the R software installed on your computer. Before going to the next step, you have to understand the definition of a vector in R. In R, a vector is simply a collection of values with the same type; it could be all `character`, `numeric`, or `logical`. For example, it could contain names of places/countries, it could contain the number of hours a person spends on the internet over the last seven days, or it could also contain whether a group of people has a certain disease or not (true/false).

How to do it...

Creating a vector in R is the most easy task.

Take a look at the following steps to learn how to create a vector in R:

1. There are several ways in which you can create a vector, but the most popular and easy way to create the vector is using the concatenate function `c()` as shown in the following code snippet:

   ```
   cVec <- c("Cricket", "Football", "Basketball", "Rugby")
   ```

2. You can store the vector by giving a name of the object; in this case, `cVec` is the object name that contains the character vector. The elements of this vector do not have any name, but you can give them a name. If the elements of a vector have a name, then it is called a "named vector". For example, you can give the name of the elements of the vector `cVec` as follows:

   ```
   cVec <- c(game1="Cricket", game2="Football",
   game3="Basketball", game4="Rugby")
   ```

3. Execute the following code to create numeric and logical vectors using the `c()` function:

   ```
   nVec <- c(1:10)
   Lvec <- c(TRUE, FALSE, FALSE, TRUE)
   ```

4. Though `c()` is the most easy and convenient way to create a vector in R, you can create a vector by generating the number or character or logical sequence using any other facilities in R, such as, creating random numbers within certain intervals, say 10 to 20, or taking random sample of letters from the set of alphabets or the output of any conditional operations. Here are some examples:

   ```
   nVec2 <- runif( n=5, min=10, max=20)  #to generate random numbers
   from Uniform distribution
   cVec2 <- sample(x=letters, size= 5, replace =  F)
   Lvec2 <- nVec2>=13
   ```

5. After creating a vector, the next step is to verify its type, that is, the data type of the vector that you have just created. To access the properties of the vector, you can use one of the following functions:
      - The `is.character()` function
      - The `is.numeric()` function
      - The `is.integer()` function
      - The `is.logical()` function

6. However, before accessing the data types, the first thing you must do is verify that the object that you have created is a vector using the `is.vector()` function. The output of this function will generate a true/false:

```
is.vector(cVec)
is.vector(nVec)
is.vector(Lvec)
is.vector(cVec2)
is.vector(nVec2)
is.vector(Lvec2)
```

   The number of elements in a vector could be as few as one, to as many as you want depending on the computer's architecture and memory. Usually, the maximum length for a vector in R for all builds could be 2^31-1, but for a 64-bit build, it could be 2^34-1.

7. After creating a vector, you might need to access a single element of the vector, and the position of that single element could be anywhere in the vector. In R, the element of the vector can be accessed by using the index number of the vector. The index ranges from 1 to the length of the vector. To access the specific element of a vector, the index needs to be supplied within a square bracket `[ ]`. Here is an example of accessing the third element of the `cVec` vector:

```
cVec[3]
```

8. You can access any number of elements from the vector by providing the index of the element inside the square bracket. In other words, to get access to multiple elements of a vector, you have to provide the index as another vector inside the square brackets as follows:

```
cVec[c(1,3,5)]
```

How it works...

A vector in R is just a collection of elements of the same data type. The concatenation function c() is just a way to organize the elements next to each other to create the collection, and eventually, it creates the vector. The other way to create the vectors is using random numbers, and taking random samples is another way of organizing the elements next to each other. Though you do not need to use the concatenation function c() for those cases, implicitly, those functions are doing the same task as that of the concatenation function.

To access the properties of an object in R, you can ask a simple question of the R object in a way that the software R understands the question. For example, is.logical(x) is a simple question you are asking the object x, that is, whether it is a logical object or not. The output of this type of question will be always logical (true/false).

The vector stores its element internally by giving it a position index. You can use that position index to extract the value of that position. You can use any combination of that position index to extract the required values from the vector. Just remember that you have to provide the position index within square brackets, such as cVec[3] or cVec[c(1,2,5)]. Then, it will return the value of the position you specified, in this case, the third element or the first, second, and fifth element of the vector.

There's more...

You can create a vector by providing a combination of character, numeric, and logical, but the output will be always a single type. Now, the question is, if you try to create a vector of mixed data types, then what will be the type of output vector? The answer follows the rules as follows:

- A combination of character and any other data type produces a character vector
- A combination of numeric and logical data type produces a numeric vector
- A combination of complex and numeric or logical data type produces a complex vector

See also

There are other ways to create a vector such as the rep() function and the sequence operator (:). To access properties, it is recommended that you inspect the mode and classes of an R object.

Creating a matrix and accessing its properties

A matrix is a two-dimensional arrangement of vectors of the same type. Like vectors in R, the matrix is restricted to one data type. In this recipe, you will learn how to create a matrix, how to access its elements, and understand a few notes on matrix operations.

Getting ready

To get started with this recipe, you must have R installed on your computer. You also need to understand the structure of a matrix and various operations. There is no library required for this recipe, but if you are interested in advanced matrix algebra, then you might consider the *See also* section of this recipe. A matrix is considered as a two-dimensional grid where each cell is represented by a row and column index and the value of the cell is the entries of the matrix. The cell may contain logical, numeric, or character elements.

How to do it...

There are several ways to create a matrix, but the most convenient way to create a matrix is through the use of the `matrix()` function from base R. Let's perform the following steps to learn about creating a matrix:

1. Execute the following code snippet that depicts a matrix of order 2 x 2 with all elements equal to 1:

```
matA <- matrix(1, nrow=2, ncol=2)
matB <- matrix(1:9, nrow=3, ncol=3, byrow=TRUE)
```

2. There are alternative ways to create a matrix, such as, binding two or more vectors to create a two-dimensional representation as follows:

```
Vec1 <- 1:3
Vec2 <- 3:1
```

3. Now, bind the preceding two vectors as two different rows to create a matrix as follows:

```
matC <- rbind(Vec1, Vec2)
```

4. Alternatively, you could bind the two vectors as a column of a matrix as follows:

```
matD <- cbind(Vec1, Vec2)
```

5. Since a matrix is a two-dimensional arrangement of vectors, you can create a matrix using the `array` function by specifying two dimensions. For example, take a look at the following code snippet:

```
matE <- array(1:9, dim=c(3,3))
```

6. Once you have created a matrix, you might want to check whether you have created a matrix based on the specification of R. To test the object, you can use the `is.matrix()` function. If the output is TRUE, then you are certain that you have created the matrix correctly:

```
is.matrix(matA)
```

7. To determin the number of rows/columns, you can use either the `nrow()` or `ncol()` function as follows:

```
nrow(matA)
ncol(matA)
```

8. You can access a specific element of a matrix by giving the row index and column index within square brackets as follows:

```
matA[1, 2]
```

9. It will give the second value of the first row and alternatively, the first value of the second column. Let's assume you omit one index and provide only the other one as follows:

```
matA[2, ]
```

Then, it will give only the values of the second row of the matrix.

How it works...

The `matrix()` function takes the input of as a vector, number of rows, number of columns, and whether the arrangement should be by row or not. The function then places the elements of the vector into a two-dimensional arrangement based on the `nrow` and `ncol` values. By default, it fills the elements column by column if `byrow` is not explicitly specified. However, if `byrow=TRUE` is specified, then the elements fill by one row at a time.

The `cbind()` and `rbind()` functions are very similar to the concatenation function `c()`, but the `cbind()` function places the vector as columns in a two-dimensional representation and `rbind()` places the vectors as rows in a two-dimensional representation to create a matrix.

The `array()` function takes two necessary inputs: one is a vector of elements and another is a vector of dimensions. If you use only two numbers in the `dim` = argument, then this function will create a matrix and the elements will be filled column by column.

There's more...

Once you have created the matrix, then you can do matrix operations that are mathematically applicable, such as, matrix addition, subtraction, multiplication, inverse calculation, and many more. Matrix addition and subtraction are very much like the addition and subtraction of two numbers, but both matrices must have the same number of rows and columns. In other words, you cannot add or subtract two matrices if their number of rows and/or columns differ. From this recipe, `matA` and `matB` are not mathematically conformable for addition or subtraction, but `matB` and `matE` are conformable to do that operation:

```
matADD <- matB + matE
```

To multiply one matrix by another matrix, the number of columns of the first matrix must be the same as of the number of rows of the second matrix. For example, the number of columns of `matA` is 2 and the number of rows in `matC` is 2, so you can multiply these two matrices as follows:

```
matMult <- matA %*% matC
```

Notice that the matrix multiplication symbol is different from the multiplication symbol of two single numbers. For matrix multiplication, you must use `%*%`.

If you use the regular multiplication symbol and both matrices have the same number of rows and columns, then it will perform element-wise multiplication. In other words, it will multiply each corresponding element and create a new matrix as follows:

```
matMult2 <- matB * matE #element-wise multiplication
matMult2 <- matB %*% matE #Matrix multiplication
```

Finally, you can also give the name of the rows and columns using the `rownames()` and `colnames()` functions as follows:

```
rownames(matA) <- c("row1", "row2")
colnames(matA) <- c("col1", "col2")
```

See also

After creating a matrix, you can do every type of matrix operation ranging from transpose, inverse, eigen value, and eigen vector calculation. It is recommended that you study any linear algebra for matrix operations, and then, you can apply those operations in R. Discussion of linear algebra is beyond the scope of this recipe.

Creating a data frame and accessing its properties

A data frame in R is also a two-dimensional arrangement like a matrix, but it can contain a combination of data types in different columns. One column could be numeric, another column could be character. A data frame can be considered as a natural generalization of a matrix in R. In this recipe, you will learn how to create a data frame and how to access various columns and/or elements of it.

Getting ready

Since you have already learned to create a matrix, it will be relatively simple to understand the data frame. It is good to have an understanding of variables and datasets. Though the structure of a data frame is similar to a matrix, it has more information within it.

How to do it...

Let's take a look at the following steps to learn how to create a data frame in R:

1. To create a data frame in R, you will have to use a function called
   `data.frame()`. This function is the convenient way to create a data frame.
   Within the `data.frame()` function, it contains the named vector that ultimately
   represents columns of the dataset. Each column's data type could be very
   different from another. For example, one column could be numeric, another
   column could be character, and the other columns could be logical. Here is an
   example of creating a small data frame object using the `data.frame()` function:

   ```
   datA <- data.frame(ID = 1:5, hourSpetOnInternet =
   c(5,3,4,1,2), GENDER = c("M", "F", "F", "M", "F"))
   ```

2. After creating the data frame, you can now check the properties of it as follows:
   - Data type of each of the columns
   - Number of rows
   - Number of columns
   - Names of the columns
   - Printing the content of the data frame
   - Printing the first and last few rows of the data frame
   - Accessing a single column

3. To determine the data types of each column, execute the following code snippet:

```
str(datA)
```

```
> str(datA)'data.frame':   5 obs. of   3 variables:
$ ID                : int   1 2 3 4 5
$ hourSpetOnInternet: num   5 3 4 1 2
$ GENDER            : Factor w/ 2 levels "F","M": 2 1 1 2 1

nrow(datA) # to know number of rows in the data frame
ncol(datA) # to know number of columns in the data frame
head(datA, n=2)  # print first 2 rows of the data frame
tail(datA, n=2) # print last 2 rows of the data frame
datA$ID # to get access to ID variable only
datA[["ID"]] # to get access to ID variable only
names(datA) # to get column names of the data frame
colnames(datA) # to get column names of the data frame
```

How it works...

The `data.frame()` function works similarly to the `cbind()` function, but it preserves data types of each of the columns. In the `cbind()` function, all the columns are converted to character if any of the columns are of character type. See the conversion rules in the earlier recipe, *Creating a vector and accessing its properties* for more details.

The other functions such as `nrow()`, `ncol()`, and `colnames()` work in the same way as they do in a matrix. The `str()` function is a special function to know the structure of the data frame. It gives the output of data types for each column, along with the first few values of the columns and column names.

To get access to a column, you can use the dollar sign `$` next to the data frame name, such as `datA$ID`, to get access to the ID column of the data frame. Similarly, you can specify the column name with double-square brackets and use quotation, for example, `datA[["ID"]]`. Moreover, the columns are implicitly indexed by serial numbers from 1 to the number of columns, for example, 1 to 3 in this case. You can get access to a column by giving the position index of the column. For example, to get access to the ID column, you can execute the following code:

```
datA[,1] # this is similar to extracting elements from a matrix
```

The other two functions `head()` and `tail()` are to print the content of the dataset from the top six and bottom six rows. If you use only `head(datA)`, by default, it will print the top six rows of the data frame.

There's more...

The `data.frame()` function has an optional argument `stringsAsFactors`, which prevents the character columns' automatic conversion into factors. A factor is another R data type that is used to represent categorical variables such as 1 for M and 2 for the F category. In the dataset that you have created using the `data.frame()` function, notice that the column GENDER is a factor type, though you did not explicitly mention it. Intuitively, the GENDER column should be a character column with values M and F. To prevent this automatic conversion, you must use `stringsAsFactors=FALSE` as follows:

```
datB <- data.frame(ID = 1:5, hourSpetOnInternet = c(5,3,4,1,2),
GENDER = c("M", "F", "F", "M", "F"), stringsAsFactors=FALSE)
```

See also

There is a way to convert a matrix to a data frame. To know more about that conversion, follow the *Converting a matrix to a data frame and a data frame to a matrix* recipe, later in this chapter.

Creating an array and accessing its properties

An array is a way to organize data of the same type in more than two dimensions. An array could be of any dimension, and the data type must be the same in each of the array elements. A matrix is a special case of an array with only two dimensions. In this recipe, you will learn how to create an array and how to access its elements.

Getting ready

Suppose you are in a situation where you must store a series of matrices into a single R object and then perform analysis based on that; however, in this case, this is the perfect and efficient way to create an array. For example, you are in a situation to store four matrices of 2 x 2 order.

How to do it...

The simplest way to create an array is to use the `array()` function from R and then specify the elements and the dimension as shown in the following code snippet:

```
arrayA <- array(1:16, dim=c(2,2,4))
```

The preceding function will produce an array of four matrices of order 2 x 2. By default, it will create the columns of the matrices and place them next to each other. The output of an array looks like this:

```
> arrayA
, , 1

     [,1] [,2]
[1,]    1    3
[2,]    2    4

, , 2

     [,1] [,2]
[1,]    5    7
[2,]    6    8

, , 3
```

```
        [,1]  [,2]
[1,]     9    11
[2,]    10    12


, , 4

        [,1]  [,2]
[1,]    13    15
[2,]    14    16
```

How it works...

To work in an array, you have to understand how the dimension works. The first and second dimensions in the preceding example specify the dimension of the matrices. Each matrix is element of this array. The third dimension specifies the element number of the array. So, to extract any matrix from this array, you have to specify the position of that matrix by providing the position index using the third dimension. For example, to extract the second matrix from the arrayA object, execute the following code:

```
arrayA2 <- arrayA[, , 2]
```

Since the value for the first and second dimensions is blank, it indicates that all of the elements have to be extracted in that direction. So, in this case, it will extract all rows and all columns of the second matrix from the arrayA object.

If you are interested in getting access to a single element from a second matrix, let's say the first element, then the code will be as follows:

```
arrayA[1,1,2]
```

There's more...

You can give a name to each dimension of an array using the optional argument dim names inside the array() function. For example, take a look at the following code snippet:

```
column.names <- c("COL1","COL2")
row.names <- c("ROW1","ROW2")
matrix.names <- c("m1","m2", "m3", "m4")
arrayB <- array(1:16, dim=c(2,2,4), dimnames =list(row.names,
column.names, matrix.names))
```

The dimension of the matrices inside an array should be the same and the data type must be the same as well.

You can also easily change the layout of the array by simply changing the dimension as follows:

```
dim(arrayA) <- c(2,4,2)
```

 The multiplication of all dimensions (2 x 4 x 2) should be the same as the total number of elements in the array.

See also

To check whether an object is an array or not, you could use the `is.array()` function. To do advanced processing and/or analysis on an array object, it is recommended that you review the `plyr` library, especially the `alply()`, `aaply()`, and `adply()` functions, because those functions take input as an array and then perform the requested operations.

Creating a list from a combination of vector, matrix, and data frame

A list is the natural generalization of a data frame in R. A data frame is a rectangular arrangement of rows and columns where each of the columns must be of the same length. A list can contain a variety of heterogeneous objects with various lengths and data types. An array contains only one data type, whereas a list could contain heterogeneous data types of various lengths. In that sense, a list is also a natural generalization of an array. A list is a versatile R object, and it is important to know how it stores elements and how you can access it. In this recipe, you will learn how to create a list and access its elements.

Getting ready

Recall that you have created several R objects in the prior recipes, such as vector, matrix, data frame, and array. Now, you are in a position to create another single R object that could contain all the objects that you have already created and then want to access those as needed. To get ready for this recipe, let's re-run those lines of code and create those objects again:

```
cVec <- c("Cricket", "Football", "Basketball", "Rugby")
nVec <- c(1:10)
Lvec <- c(TRUE, FALSE, FALSE, TRUE)
matA <- matrix(1, nrow=2, ncol=2)
datA <- data.frame(ID = 1:5, hourSpetOnInternet = c(5,3,4,1,2),
GENDER = c("M", "F", "F", "M", "F"))
arrayA <- array(1:16, dim=c(2,2,4))
```

In this recipe, you will organize these heterogeneous objects into a single R object that is called `list`.

How to do it...

Let's perform the following steps to create a list:

1. The `list()` R function is used to create a list object. The dimension of a list could be any, and it can contain heterogeneous objects. To create a list called `listA`, execute the following code:

```
listA <- list(cVec, nVec, Lvec, matA, datA, arrayA)
```

2. The list could be a named list or without a name. To create a named list, the syntax is similar to the creation of a named vector. Here is an example:

```
listB <- list(vector1 = cVec, vector2 = nVec, vector3 = Lvec,
matrix1 = matA, data1 = datA, array1 = arrayA)
```

3. The list preserves the original properties of the elements. To check the properties at a glance, you can use the `str()` function as follows:

```
str(listA)
str(listB)
```

The preceding function will then provide the output of the number of elements of the list, data types of each of the components, and the name of each component (if there is any), along with few values of the components, as follows:

```
> str(listA)
List of 6
 $ : chr [1:4] "Cricket" "Football" "Basketball" "Rugby"
 $ : int [1:10] 1 2 3 4 5 6 7 8 9 10
 $ : logi [1:4] TRUE FALSE FALSE TRUE
 $ : num [1:2, 1:2] 1 1 1 1
 $ :'data.frame': 5 obs. of  3 variables:
  ..$ ID              : int [1:5] 1 2 3 4 5
  ..$ hourSpetOnInternet: num [1:5] 5 3 4 1 2
  ..$ GENDER          : Factor w/ 2 levels "F","M": 2 1 1 2 1
 $ : int [1:2, 1:2, 1:4] 1 2 3 4 5 6 7 8 9 10 ...
```

How it works...

The `list()` function works just like the concatenation function `c()`. It places each of the elements next to each other, while preserving their original data types and names of the objects. To get access to the component of a list, the simplest way is to use the double-square brackets along with a sequential index number of the element position as follows:

```
listA[[1]]
```

The preceding function will give the output of the first element of the list, which is a character vector of four elements, as follows:

```
[1] "Cricket"    "Football"   "Basetball" "Rugby"
```

You can use the dollar $ operator next to the name of the list object to extract elements from the list. However, the list object must be a named list; otherwise the $ operator will not work. For example, to extract the data frame from `listB`, execute the following code snippet:

```
listB$data1

> listB$data1
ID hourSpetOnInternet GENDER
 1  1                  5      M
 2  2                  3      F
 3  3                  4      F
 4  4                  1      M
 5  5                  2      F
```

There's more...

If the length of each of the elements is the same, then it can be converted into a data frame. Also, if all lengths are the same and each of the component's data types are the same, then it can be converted into a matrix.

See also

If you want to convert objects among list, data frame, and matrix, then you could use the following functions:

- `as.list()`
- `as.data.frame()`
- `as.matrix()`

Converting a matrix to a data frame and a data frame to a matrix

A matrix is a two-dimensional arrangement of data with rows and columns where each row/column is of the same data type, either all numeric, all character, or all logical. Moreover, the number of elements in each column should be the same, and the number of elements in each row should also be the same.

A data frame is also a two-dimensional arrangement of data with rows and columns, but each column could be of very different types; for example, a data frame may contain both character and numeric columns. However, the number of elements in each column should be the same. Since both data structures share some common properties, they could be converted from one structure to another. In this recipe, you will learn to convert a matrix to a data frame and a data frame to a matrix.

Getting ready

To convert a matrix to a data frame and a data frame to a matrix, first, create a matrix and a data frame to get started, as follows:

```
M1 <- matrix(1:9, nrow=3, ncol= 3, byrow=TRUE)
D1 <- data.frame(x1= c(1,3,2,4,5), x2= c("Cricket", "Football",
"Basketball", "Rugby", "Baseball" ))
```

How to do it...

The object conversion in R is very intuitive and easy to understand. The name of the function itself tells the story. Let's perform the following steps to convert a matrix to a data frame and a data frame to a matrix:

1. To convert a matrix to a data frame, the `as.data.frame()` function is enough:

    ```
    M1ToData <- as.data.frame(M1)
    ```

2. To check whether the newly created object `M1ToData` is a data frame or not, you can use either the `class()` function or the `str()` function. The `str()` function will give the results along with the type of each column. The output of the `str()` function is as follows:

    ```
    > str(M1ToData)
    'data.frame':        3 obs. of  3 variables:
     $ V1: int  1 4 7
     $ V2: int  2 5 8
     $ V3: int  3 6 9
    ```

3. Notice that the columns got new names such as V1, V2, and V3 because a data frame must have a name for each column. If there is no name specified, then the default name will be V1, V2, and so on. To convert a data frame to a matrix, execute the following code snippet:

    ```
    D1ToMatrix <- as.matrix(D1)
    > str(D1ToMatrix)
     chr [1:5, 1:2] "1" "3" "2" "4" "5" "Cricket" "Football"
     "Basketball" "Rugby" "Baseball"
     - attr(*, "dimnames")=List of 2
      ..$ : NULL
      ..$ : chr [1:2] "x1" "x2"
    ```

    Since one of the columns of the data frame was of character type, the resultant matrix is converted to character type. The resultant matrix is a matrix of five rows and two columns. Since the conversion has been done from a data frame and each column had a name on it, the matrix also contains those column names as follows:

    ```
    colnames(D1ToMatrix)
    > colnames(D1ToMatrix)
    [1] "x1" "x2"
    ```

How it works...

The conversion from a matrix to a data frame works simply by assigning column names and then assigning the class property as `data.frame`. Since a matrix only contains one data type, the resultant data frame also contains only one data type.

The conversion of a data frame to a matrix with heterogeneous data types works a bit differently. First, it converts all columns into higher and more general data types as follows:

- A combination of character and any other data type produces a character vector
- A combination of numeric and logical data type produces a numeric vector
- A combination of complex and numeric or logical data type produces a complex vector

Then, it keeps only one type of data because a matrix is restricted to only one data type. Also, during the conversion, it preserves the column names, which can be accessed by the `colnames()` function.

There's more...

The `as.x()` function is a kind of generic function. All of the conversion between objects happens using the function `as.x()`, where x could be a list, a `data.frame`, a numeric, or logical.

See also

Learn more about the `class()`, `mode()`, and all the functions in the format `as.x()` for conversion between objects.

3
Writing Customized Functions

In this chapter, you will learn to write your own customized functions, and understand how to work with various data types within a function and access an output of a function. This chapter contain the following recipes:

- Writing your first function in R
- Writing functions with multiple arguments and use of default values
- Handling data types in input arguments
- Producing different output types and return values
- Making a recursive call to a function
- Handling exceptions and error messages

Introduction

A function in R is a set of instructions to do a certain task based on the input provided. There are lots of default functions in R to carry out data processing, analysis, and visualization tasks. However, you might require your own customized function to carry out a task that is not available within the default functions, for example, you are proposing a new algorithm to detect extreme values from a dataset and the algorithm is not yet available as a default function or not yet available as an R library. In this situation, you must write your own function, giving all the instructions to your algorithm to carry out extreme value detection task.

There are default R functions available to carry out descriptive statistical analysis such as calculating mean, standard deviation, median, and other similar values. However, you may be in a situation where you want all the values over many groups. You could do this task by performing individual calculation for each group separately, but it will be time consuming. To do the same task efficiently, a customized function could be very useful.

In this chapter, you will write your own customized function and learn how to work with input and output.

Writing your first function in R

A function in R is a set of instructions for a certain task to complete. The function could take any input you define, or it could work without any input. In this recipe, you will learn how to write a function and you will learn about the components of a function.

Getting ready

Let's say you want to calculate the ratio of the standard deviation and mean of a given vector of five numbers. The input values are (3, 7, 2, 6, 9). To give these five values as an input to a function, you need to create a vector that contains these numbers as follows:

```
V1 <- c(3, 7, 2, 6, 9)
```

How to do it...

To write a function, the first and most important thing is the name of the function. Let's perform the following steps to write your first function in R:

1. You must give a name to the new function that you are going to write. The name of the function must start with a character. The function name could start with a dot (.) or with an underscore (_). Now, let's give the name of the new function for this recipe as fsdByMean:

```
fsdByMean <- function(vectorInput){
  average <- mean(vectorInput)
  std <- sd(vectorInput)
  stdByMean <- std/average
  return(stdByMean)
}
```

2. Now, to use the function, you should call it as follows:

```
fsdByMean(vectorInput = V1)
[1] 0.5335133
```

How it works...

To write a function in R, there is a keyword in R called `function`. Using this keyword, you can write any type of customized function in R. In this recipe, the task is as follows:

1. Write a function that will take a numeric vector as input.
2. Then, it will calculate the mean and standard deviation internally.
3. Finally, it will give an output of the ratio of the standard deviation and mean.

Each of the input parameters is called the argument of a function. In this recipe, the input argument is `vectorInput`. You can use any numeric input vector to specify the input of this function by passing the argument as `vectorInput=V1`.

Within the curly braces, the actual calculation happened. In this case, the mean and standard deviation has been calculated separately and then the ratio of the standard deviation and mean has been calculated and stored into another object called `stdByMean`. The `return` keyword instructs the function to give an output from the function to the R console. Whatever object names are given inside the `return` keyword, it will provide that value as an output of the function. In this example, the function will return the value of the `stdByMean` object. The other two values that have been calculated internally (mean and standard deviation) will not be available as output. To call a function, the proper code is as follows:

```
nameOfFunction(argument1=value)
```

By following this convention, you could call the new function as follows:

```
fsdByMean(vectorInput = V1)
```

The preceding function generates the following output:

```
> fsdByMean(vectorInput = V1)
[1] 0.5335133
```

There's more...

Whatever calculation has been done within primary curly braces, all of those are only for internal use, which means, within the function. If you want the internal value as output, then you must specify that object into the `return` statement. For example, if you want the mean of the input vector as output from the function, then you can simply change the `return` statement as follows:

```
fsdByMean <- function(vectorInput){
 average <- mean(vectorInput)
 std <- sd(vectorInput)
 stdByMean <- std/average
 return(average)
}

> fsdByMean(vectorInput = V1)
[1] 5.4
```

The name of the function and other internal calculation remains the same, but the output will be different just because of the `return` statement.

Writing functions with multiple arguments and use of default values

The input of a function is known as an **argument**. Often, you may need to write a customized function with multiple inputs. In this recipe, you will learn to use multiple arguments and the default values of the argument.

Getting ready

In this recipe, you will write a new customized function that will take more than one input, and at least one of them will contain default values. Specifically, in this recipe, the function will take one numeric vector as input and another character input with a default value. The objective of this function is to calculate descriptive statistics of the numeric vector, and another character input will specify the type of descriptive statistics, either classical or robust.

The classical descriptive statistics here refers to mean and standard deviation, whereas the robust counterpart refers to median and **median absolute deviation** (**MAD**).

The input numeric vector is given as follows:

```
V1 <- c(3, 7, 2, 6, 9)
```

The character input is given by `type= "classical"` as the default value, but if you specify `type= "robust"`, it will act accordingly.

How to do it...

Let's say the name of the function is `fDescriptive`. The prefix `f` in the name of the function is just for convenience so that you can easily identify that this object is a function. The name of the first argument could be any valid object name. In this recipe, the numeric input argument is defined by `numVec`, and the second argument is defined as `type`. Now, the function can be written as follows:

```
fDescriptive <- function(numVec, type = "classical"){
  avg <- mean(numVec)
  std <- sd(numVec)
  med <- median(numVec)
  medad <- mad(numVec)
  out1 <- c(mean = avg, sd = std)
  out2 <-c(median = med, mad = medad)
  if(type== "classical")
    return(out1)
  else if (type == "robust")
    return(out2)
}
```

How it works...

The multiple-argument function works as it works for a single argument. After giving the name of the function, the statements within curly braces do all the internal calculation. This function takes the numeric vector as input by the `numVec` argument, and also, the second argument `type` = specifies the type of summary statistics to be calculated.

After taking the input numeric vector, the function does the following things:

1. It internally calculates all the required statistics such as mean, standard deviation, median, and median absolute deviation.
2. It stores all the calculated values into different objects; in this case, `avg` contains mean, `std` contains standard deviation, `med` contains median, and `medad` contains median absolute deviation.
3. Then, the function organizes the output for classical and robust options by the `out1` and `out2` objects.
4. Once all the calculations have been done, the function checks the type of output to be returned based on the value provided by the `type` = argument.
5. If there is nothing explicitly specified by the `type=` argument, then by default, it will return classical descriptive statistics, that is, mean and standard deviation, because the default value of the `type` argument is `classical`.
6. To override classical output, you have to instruct the function explicitly that an output type will be `robust`, so `type= "robust"` has to be specified. So, ultimately, you will use this function to get classical descriptive statistics as the output as follows:

```
> fDescriptive(numVec = V1)
     mean          sd
5.400000 2.880972
```

The preceding function can be used in the following way as well:

```
> fDescriptive(numVec = V1, type = "classical")
mean          sd
5.400000 2.880972
```

7. Both the preceding calls will give classical descriptive statistics as output. To get robust output such as, median and median absolute deviation, execute the following code:

```
fDescriptive(numVec = V1, type = "robust")
```

There's more...

Any function in R with either a single argument or multiple arguments works similarly. The only difference is the internal calculation and the use of arguments. In this function, the `type` argument takes only two values, but there is no way to check the input. For example, if someone mistakenly wrote `type = "Robust"`, then the function will not provide any output. R is case sensitive, so `robust` and `Robust` are treated very differently.

To handle this ambiguity, you can write a few extra statements within the function body. The extra statement is to convert the `type` input into either all lowercase or all uppercase so that it works for both `Robust` and `robust`. Following are the lines of code that are needed in the body of the function to handle this situation:

```
type = tolower(type)
```

Finally, if you provide any other value in the `type` argument, then the function will not return any output. For example, if you type `type = "rstat"`, it will not give any output.

Handling data types in input arguments

There are different data types in R, such as character, numeric, and logical. These three are the most important data types in R. When creating a function in R, the mix of data types could create a problem and eventually the result will not be as expected. In this recipe, you will learn how to check the data types inside a function and how to convert them if necessary.

Getting ready

In this recipe, you will write the same function as you wrote in the previous recipe, *Writing functions with multiple arguments and use of default values* of this chapter. The `fDescriptive` function takes one numeric vector as input and one character vector as the second input. In this recipe, you will write some statements to check the types of required input for the `fDescriptive` function.

How to do it...

To check the input data types, the required function is is.x, where x is a placeholder for character, numeric, logical, vector, matrix, and so on. Using this function, the data type and data structure can be easily assessed. You will use the is.x type of function in the body of the fDescriptive function as follows:

```
fDescriptive <- function(numVec, type = "classical"){
  type <- tolower(type)
  if(is.numeric(numVec) & is.vector(numVec)){
    avg <- mean(numVec)
    std <- sd(numVec)
    med <- median(numVec)
    medad <- mad(numVec)
    out1 <- c(mean = avg, sd = std)
    out2 <-c(median = med, mad = medad)
    if(type== "classical")
      return(out1)
    else if (type == "robust")
      return(out2)
  }
}
```

How it works...

The default R function of the form is.x is very powerful and it is easy to understand to check data types and data structure. The use of this type of function is very important to ensure correct input into a function. In this recipe, the newly written function fDescriptive is expected to take a numeric vector as input and do the rest of the calculation. The user might mistakenly provide wrong input and, eventually, the function will provide the wrong output. To avoid receiving a wrong output, you must use the is.x function to check the input.

Inside the body of the function, the use of is.numeric() and is.vector() functions ensures that the input is a numeric vector, and then it calculates the necessary statistics for output. If either of these two checks fail, then the function will not provide any output at all.

There's more...

During input validation you could generate customized messages so that anyone can see what was wrong. The exception handling has been discussed in detail into the recipe *Handling exceptions and error messages* in this chapter. There are functions such as `warning()`, `stop()`, `tryCatch()`, and so on which have been discussed with proper examples.

Producing different output types and return values

Based on the requirement of the user, sometimes you may need to produce an output of different data types. You might need to perform a numeric calculation inside the function, but an output needs to display as a text or sometimes, the input is numeric but the output is a customized graph. There are several types of output that can be produced by creating customized function; also, the values of the output can be controlled. In this recipe, you will write a new function that can produce diffeent types of output.

Getting ready

In this recipe, you will write a very small customized function that will calculate the mean and standard error of the mean and provide an output as a character string. The objective is to introduce the data type conversion during output extraction from a function. Let's say, you are given the following input vector:

```
V1 <- c(3, 7, 2, 6, 9)
```

How to do it...

Let's start with the function name `meanSe` to write the function. Here is the complete code of the function:

```
meanSe <- function(numVec){
  if(is.numeric(numVec) & is.vector(numVec)){
    avg <- mean(numVec)
    std <- sd(numVec)
    se <- std/sqrt(length(numVec))
    out <- paste("Mean of the input vector is = ",
         paste(avg), " with a standard error = ",
```

```
            paste(se),  sep = "")
       return(out)
    }
  }
```

How it works...

The type of output produced by the object is created or mentioned inside the `return` statement. If you want a character type output, then you must supply a character type object inside the `return` statement. In this recipe, the `meanSe` function calculates the mean and standard deviation, and then, it converts it into a character object by the following code lines:

```
out <- paste("Mean of the input vector is = ",
       paste(avg), " with a standard error = ",
       paste(se), sep = "")
```

The `paste` function here has been used to print the text and convert the numeric output into character type. The `out` object contains a line of text with the value of mean and standard deviation in it.

There's more...

An output data type could be one of the many available data types in R, and you could organize the output into a different data structure. For example, the output of this function can be returned as a list of two named elements by creating the function as follows:

```
meanSe <- function(numVec){
  if(is.numeric(numVec) & is.vector(numVec)){
    avg <- mean(numVec)
    std <- sd(numVec)
    se <- std/sqrt(length(numVec))
    out <- list(mean = avg, standardError = se)
    return(out)
  }
}
```

Making a recursive call to a function

Recursion usually indicates repetition. In the data analysis journey, you might need to use a single function multiple times to do a task such as calculating summary statistics for each column in a dataset. Sometimes, you might need to write a function in such a way that you need to use the function itself within that function. In this recipe, you will learn both how to use a function for multiple columns or rows in a data frame and how to write a function that can call the function itself.

Getting ready

This recipe has two parts. The first part is to use a function on a different subset or rows or columns of a data frame. The second part of this recipe is to write a function that can call itself within the body of the function.

In the repetition part, you will calculate robust descriptive statistics for each column of a data frame, let's say the default `iris` data, using the function you have written in the earlier recipe, *Writing functions with multiple arguments and use of default values*, in this chapter.

In the recursion part, you will write a function that can call the function itself. In this part, you will write a function to calculate the sum of a finite series such as $1\^3 + 2\^3 + \ldots + n\^3$.

How to do it...

Let's take a look at the following two parts:

- **The repetition part**: Let's take a look at the following steps to get a clear picture of the repetition part:
    1. Let's first rewrite the `fDescriptive` function as follows:

    ```
    fDescriptive <- function(numVec, type = "classical"){
      avg <- mean(numVec)
      std <- sd(numVec)
      med <- median(numVec)
      medad <- mad(numVec)
      out1 <- c(mean = avg, sd = std)
      out2 <-c(median = med, mad = medad)
      if(type== "classical")
        return(out1)
      else if (type == "robust")
    ```

```
        return(out2)
   }
```

2. Now, using the function, you will calculate robust descriptive statistics for four columns of the `iris` dataset, a default dataset of flowers in R. This dataset has four numeric variables and one categorical variable:

```
robustSummary <- apply(X = iris[,-5], MARGIN = 2, FUN =
fDescriptive, type = "robust")
```

- **The recursion part**: Let's take a look at the following steps to get a clear picture of the recursion part:
    1. The objective is to write a function to calculate the sum of a cubic series such as 1^3 + 2^3 + ... +n^3 using the recursion technique. Let's give the function name as `cubicSum`; you will use the `cubicSum` function within the body of this function as follows:

```
cubicSum <- function(n){
  if(n==0)
     return(0)
  else
     return(n^3 + cubicSum(n-1))
}
```

    2. The use of the function is as follows:

```
cubicSum(n = 3)
```

How it works...

Let's take a look at how each of these two parts works individually:

- **The repetition part**: The `apply()` function is a default function for repeatedly using a function to do the same task over different rows or columns of a data frame. In this case, the `iris` dataset has four numeric columns and the objective is to calculate the median and MAD of those four columns using a customized function. Since the dataset has more than one column but the customized function `fDescriptive` can take only the numeric vector of input, this is a repetition problem. The argument of the `apply()` function works as follows:
    - X: This is either a matrix or a data frame to which the targeted operation will be performed

- MARGIN: This is to specify whether the operation will be row wise or column wise; here, MARGIN = 2 indicates that the operation will be column wise
- FUN: This is to specify what function to use repeatedly over each of the columns in the dataset
- type: This is an additional argument that comes from the fDescriptive function, and you must supply the value of this argument explicitly

Once all the input is specified correctly, it will calculate the required statistics and stores those statistics in the robustSummary object.

Note that, in X = iris[,-5], a negative 5 has been used to exclude the character column from the iris dataset.

- **Recursion part**: The objective of this function is to calculate the sum of a cubic series using the recursion technique. The function works as follows:
    - The function takes the nth value as the input by the argument n=
    - If n = 0, then the output will be 0
    - If the value of n > 0, then it calculates the cubic value of the nth element of the series and then calls the function itself with (n-1) and then adds the result with the nth cubic value
    - The process continues until you get n = 0
    - If you use n = 3, then it calculates the sum as follows:
        - The input n = 3 is greater than 0, so n^3 + cubicSum(n-1) == > 27 + cubicSum(2) ==>27 + 2^3 + cubicsSum(2-1) ==> 35 + cubicSum(1) = 36

There's more...

There are many functions available in different libraries for doing repetition tasks, such as, plyr, dplyr, and the family of the apply() functions such as apply(), sapply(), and lapply(). These functions are alternatives of a for loop. In R, a for loop is slower than any one of these alternative functions.

For the recursive call of a function, `do.call()` is one of the popular choices, but this also works just like repetition tasks.

Handling exceptions and error messages

Whenever you are creating a function, there could be a conditional statement or even some mathematical operation that might not be executable for all situations. For example, if you are transforming a numeric vector into logarithms, then a negative value will give an error. In this recipe, you will learn how to handle exceptions and errors and/or warnings while you write your own customized functions. There are several functions in R to handle exceptions/errors/warnings as follows:

- `warning()`: This function can generate a warning message
- `stop()`: This function can generate an error message
- `supressWarnings(expr)`: This function evaluates the expression inside the function and then ignores warnings if there are any
- `tryCatch()`: This function (`tryCatch()` or `try()`) evaluates the code inside the parenthesis and then assigns an exception handler

In this recipe, you will learn how to use an exception handler by creating your function.

Getting ready

Suppose you are transforming a numeric vector into its logarithmic counterpart. For example, you are given the `V1` vector to transform into logarithms:

```
V1 <- c(3, 7, -2, 6, 9, 0, -4)
```

The objective is to take the logarithm of `V1`. Notice that `V1` contains a negative number and zero, which will generate an error. In this recipe, you will handle the exception using the exception handler options available in R.

How to do it...

Let's write the function with the error handler implemented inside the body of the function. There are several ways to handle the exception, using the following steps:

1. Let's take a look at the use of the `stop()` function in the following code snippet:

    ```
    logX <- function(numVec1){
      if(any(numVec1<0))
        stop("A negative value exists")
      else logV1 <- log(numVec1)
      return(logV1)
    }
    ```

2. Let's take a look at the use of the `try()` function in the following code snippet:

    ```
    logX1 <- function(numVec1){
      try(logV1 <- log(numVec1))
      return(logV1)
    }
    ```

3. Let's take a look at the use of the `tryCatch()` function in the following code snippet:

    ```
    logX2 <- function(numVec1){
      tryCatch(
        return(logV1 <- log(numVec1)),
        warning = function(w) print("A negative input occurred"))
    }
    ```

How it works...

The objective was to take the logarithm of a given numeric vector that contains a zero and negative numbers. The function is implemented in the following three different ways and their outputs are different:

*   `stop()`: This function generates a customized error message based on the condition supplied. In this example, the condition was to look for any number less than or equal to zero. If there is such a number, then the function will print the error message as, "A negative value exists", and the function will stop producing any other output. Finally, the only error message will be displayed on the R console.

- `try()`: This function has been used to handle an exception situation. This function tests the expression inside the `try()` block of the code. If any exception occurs, then it passes that argument and continues to execute the rest of the tasks. In the end, it issues a warning message. So, the output of the `try()` function will be the logarithm of the input vector that are non-zero positive numbers and `NaN` and/or -Inf for zero and negative numbers, along with the warning message `In log(numVec1) : NaNs produced`. So, the `try()` function will produce the output where the exception did not occur.
- `tryCatch()`: This function has been used to handle the exception. This function works very similarly to the `stop()` function, but you do not need to write the condition to test the input vector. It will automatically check for an exceptional situation, and if there is any, then it will display the customized warning or error message as implemented. Also, this function will not produce any output if there is any exception.

There's more...

In the `tryCatch()` option, if the exception happens, then it executes all the subsequent lines but it only returns the result of the exception by giving error or warning messages. The important thing in the `tryCatch()` function is that you are able to replace the exception by providing the correct operation inside the `tryCatch()` function.

See also

There are some very good resources available to further study exception handling. Here are some web links for further investigation on this topic:

- http://adv-r.had.co.nz/Exceptions-Debugging.html
- https://www.r-bloggers.com/error-handling-in-r/
- http://mazamascience.com/WorkingWithData/?p=912

4
Conditional and Iterative Operations

In this chapter, you will use conditional and repetition operators in R. This chapter covers the following recipes:

- The use of the if conditional statement
- The use of the if...else conditional operator
- The use of the ifelse vectorised conditional operator
- Writing a function using the switch operator
- Comparing the performance of switch and series of the if...else statements
- Using for loop for iterations
- Vectorised operation versus for loop

Introduction

Conditional statements and repeated operations are some of the important aspects in any programming, whether it is in the data science area or for general programming purpose. Often, you will need to test several alternative statements. For example, if you are optimizing any mathematical function, the stopping rule depends on the conditional statement. Also, if you are solving any equation that needs iteration, you must use the repetition operator. The recipes of this chapter will give you a basic understanding of the use of conditional and repetitive statements in R. Each recipe contains certain context and code with explanation. You will feel confident in writing a conditional statement and using a loop in R after reading this chapter.

The use of the if conditional statement

The use of a conditional statement or conditional operator is an essential part of any programming task. You may need to test a scenario in which there are two alternative options. Further work will depend on the outcome of the test scenario. In R, using the `if` statement, you can compare scenarios that usually have two alternative options. In this recipe, you will use the conditional statement `if`.

Getting ready

The general structure of the `if` statement in R is as follows:

```
if(test_scenario){
   valid_R_statements
   ...
}
```

From the general structure of the `if` statement, it is intuitive that if the test scenario produces `TRUE`, then the statement with curly braces will be executed; otherwise, nothing will happen.

Let's consider a situation where you have a vector of either numeric or character and you want to check whether there is any missing value or not. If any missing value exists, then you intend to print the position index of the missing value and then the number of the missing value in that input vector. Take a look at the vectors in the following code snippet:

```
x <- c(13, 21, 19, NA, 21, 16, 21, NA, 17, 18)
y<- c("Football", "Cricket", NA, "Rugby")
```

How to do it...

To check if there is any missing value in any input vector in R, you could use the `is.na()` function. This is a very useful and intuitive function to check for missing values. Now, your objective is to check whether any missing value exists in the vectors `x` and `y`. You then need to print the location of the missing value. Here is the use of the `if` statement:

```
if(any(is.na(x))){
   cat("There are missing values in x at \n")
   which(is.na(x))
}

if(any(is.na(y))){
```

```
    cat("There are missing values in y at \n")
    which(is.na(y))
}
```

How it works...

Inside the `if()` statement, the test scenario `any(is.na(x))` produces `TRUE` or `FALSE` depending on the input vector x. If the test scenario is `TRUE`, then the output will be a line of text `There are missing values in x`. Now, print the location index of the missing values.

The `which()` function searches for the position index where `is.na(x)` is `TRUE` and returns the value for that position. The `cat()` function prints the text in the R console. Similar code has been used for the character vector y too. In fact, to check missing values for any input, either numeric or character `is.na()` works fine. The output will look as follows:

```
There are missing values in x
[1]  4 8

There are missing values in x
[1]  3
```

There's more...

The `is.na()` function produces an output whose length is the same as that of the input x, but the `if()` statement works only with the test scenario that has an output of length one, either `TRUE` or `FALSE`. Now, you might think about how the vector valued `is.na()` has been used within the `if` statement.

Notice that there is another function `any()` that has been used, and this function takes the input from the output generated by `is.na()`. The `any()` function searches for a single item within the output of `is.na()`, which is `TRUE`, and eventually it generates an output of the test scenario of length one.

If you do not use the `any()` function with `if` in this example, then you will see this warning message:

```
> if(is.na(x)){
+    cat("There are missing values in x at \n")
+    which(is.na(x))
+ }

Warning message:
In if (is.na(x)) { :
  the condition has length > 1 and only the first element will be
  used
```

So, whenever you use the `if` statement, make sure that your test scenario generate only `TRUE` or `FALSE` with length 1.

The use of the if...else conditional operator

The general structure of an `if...else` statement is as follows:

```
if (conditional_expression) {
   body_of_task
} else {
   body_of_task2
}
```

The general structure is clearly intuitive to understand. If the conditional expression produces a result that is `TRUE`, then it will execute the `body_of_task` section, and if the conditional expression is `FALSE`, then it will execute the `body_of_task2` section. In this recipe, you will implement a small task to implement the `if...else` statement.

Getting ready

Unlike the `ifelse` function, `if...else` works for conditioning on a scalar-valued input and output. The `ifelse` function takes the input as a vector and produces a vector output with the same length as that of the input. However, `if...else` takes only a scalar-valued input and it only generates `TRUE` or `FALSE` and then executes the body of task that you define. Let's assume you have a number stored in the variable `a` and you want to test whether the given number is odd or even. In this recipe, you will write R code to test the `a` variable. The value of `a` could be any arbitrary integer number.

How to do it...

To check whether the value of the a variable is an even or odd number, the R code is as follows:

```
a <- 9
if(a %% 2==0){
  print("This is an even number")
} else {
  print("This is an odd number")
}
```

To check whether a given number is an odd or even, first, you must calculate the remainder after dividing the number by 2. Then, if the remainder is a 0, the number is an even number, otherwise it is an odd number.

How it works...

In the preceding code, first it calculates the remainder within the if statement and compares the result with a zero. If the output of this conditional statement returns TRUE, then the code will print This is an even number; otherwise it will print This is an odd number. So, whenever you run the preceding code, the output will be as follows:

```
> a <- 9
> if(a %% 2==0){
+   print("This is an even number")
+ } else {
+     print("This is an odd number")
+ }
[1] "This is an odd number"
```

There's more...

This is a very simple implementation of the conditional statement where the if statement part takes a scalar-valued input and produces a scalar-valued output with either TRUE or FALSE. Once the conditional statement returns its value, it executes the body of the code.

The most important thing to notice in this `if ...else` code block is the use of curly braces. If you misplaced the curly braces just before the `else` keyword, then it will produce an error as follows:

```
if(a %% 2==0){
 print("This is an even number")
}
else {
 print("This is an odd number")
}
```

The corresponding console output is given as follows:

```
> a <- 9
> if(a %% 2==0){
+   print("This is an even number")
+ }
> else {
Error: unexpected 'else' in "else"
>       print("This is an odd number")
[1] "This is an odd number"
> }
Error: unexpected '}' in "}"
```

To avoid the error, you must follow the basic structure of the `if...else` statement outlined in the introduction section of this recipe.

The use of the ifelse vectorised conditional operator

Whenever you need to compare something in two states, either true or false, then the `if` statement is the most appropriate method to use. For example, suppose you are working in a dataset and you need to transform a numeric variable into another binary variable based on a fix cut-off value. This is the most typical situation where you want to test the condition and then perform the transformation. If the condition is true, then you will go for one action, and if the condition is false, then you will go for an alternative action. In this recipe, you will see an example of this type of situation with implementation.

Getting ready

To implement this recipe, you only need a single numeric variable and a cut-off value to execute the conditional statement. Let's say you have the following variable with the values representing the number of hours spent on social media in a week:

```
x <- c(13, 21, 19, 18, 21, 16, 21, 24, 17, 18, 12, 18, 29, 17, 18,
11, 13, 20, 25, 18, 15, 19, 21, 21, 7, 12, 23, 31, 16, 19, 23, 15,
25, 19, 15, 25, 25, 16, 29, 15, 26, 29, 23, 24, 20, 19, 14, 27,
22, 26)
```

The cut-off value is the median of the given variable. The objective is to create a new variable as follows: The value of the new variable is 1 if the value of given variable is greater than median; otherwise, it is 0. Before writing the code for the recipe, you must understand the following conditional operators:

- The greater than operator (>)
- The less than operator (<)
- The greater than equal to operator (>=)
- The less than equal to operator (<=)
- The logical equal operator (==)
- The logical not equal operator (!=)
- The NOT operator (!)
- The OR operator (|)
- The AND operator (&)

How to do it...

Let's take a look at the use of the `ifelse` statement by performing the following steps:

1. Create the variable x as a numeric object in R using the concatenation function `c()` as follows:

```
x <- c(13, 21, 19, 18, 21, 16, 21, 24, 17, 18, 12, 18, 29, 17,
18, 11, 13, 20, 25, 18, 15, 19, 21, 21, 7, 12, 23, 31, 16, 19,
23, 15, 25, 19, 15, 25, 25, 16, 29, 15, 26, 29, 23, 24, 20,
19, 14, 27, 22, 26)
```

2. Now, calculate the cut-off value median as follows:

```
medX <- median(x)
medX # to see the value of median in R console
[1] 19
```

3. Create the new variable `newX` using a conditional statement as follows:

```
newX <- ifelse(x>medX,1,0)
newX  # Print the value of new variable into R console
[1] 0 1 0 0 1 0 1 1 0 0 0 1 0 0 0 1 1 0 0 0 1 1 0 0 1 1 0 0
1 0 1 0 0 1 1 0 1 0 1 1 1 1 0 0 1 1 1
```

How it works...

In the first step, you should create the source variable to apply the conditional operation and then calculate the cut-off median for this recipe. Once you have the source variable and the cut-off value, you can pass the conditional operator > inside the `ifelse` function. The `ifelse` function takes the source variable as input and a cut-off with conditional operator. In this recipe, the conditional operator is a greater than operator >. If the value of the variable x is greater than the median of x, then the new variable `newX` will get a value 1; otherwise, it will get 0. The `ifelse` function works in a vector of input, and it does not require any repetition or loop. Only the single line of code can perform the operation for the entire vector.

There's more...

There are other alternative ways to apply conditional operation in R. The `ifelse` function is one of them. The type of transformation you have done in this recipe can be done in a different way using a combination of a simple `if` statement and a loop. The details of `if` with a loop will be explained in the *Using for loop for iterations* recipe later in this chapter.

See also

To read more about the `ifelse` function and its uses, follow `https://www.r-bloggers.com/on-the-ifelse-function/`.

Writing a function using the switch operator

While writing a program, you might encounter a situation where you have to pick an item from a list based on a certain value of a test condition. The `switch` operator or the `switch` function in R is very handy in this type of situation. In this recipe, you will learn how to write R using the `switch` function.

Getting ready

Suppose you are working on a problem where you have a series of numeric variables and your task is to produce the most appropriate summary statistics for all of them. If the distribution is symmetric, then you will produce the mean and standard deviation. However, if the distribution is not symmetric, then your task is to calculate the median and MAD. In this type of situation, the use of the `switch` operator comes into play. To execute the whole task, there is a part where you will test whether the distribution is symmetric or not. Let's say you have defined a variable `sym`. This variable will take a value 1 if the distribution is symmetric, and it will take a value 2 if the distribution is not symmetric. Then, based on this variable, the summary statistics will be calculated.

In this recipe, you will use the `switch` function to define another two different functions to calculate the appropriate summary statistics. The function for summary statistics will be as follows:

1. `function(x) c(mean = mean(x), std = sd(x))`
2. `function(x) c(med= median(x), mad= mad(x))`

Based on the value of the variable `sym`, the `switch` operator will return either of the preceding two functions for later use.

How to do it...

Let's take a look at the following steps to learn about writing R using the `switch` function:

1. The general structure of the `switch` function in R is as follows:

   ```
   switch(statement, list)
   ```

2. Here, statement refers to the test condition and list refers to the list of tasks to complete. Here is the code to produce appropriate summary statistics as defined in the introduction section of this recipe:

```
sym <- 1
switch(sym, function(x) c(mean=mean(x), std=sd(x)),function(x)
c(med=median(x), mad=mad(x)))
```

3. Now, use the output of the switch function and calculate the summary statistics of any given numeric vector as follows:

```
Fun1 <- switch(sym, function(x) c(mean=mean(x), std=sd(x)),
function(x) c(med=median(x), mad=mad(x)))
x <- c(13, 21, 19, 18, 21, 16, 21, 24, 17, 18, 12, 18, 29, 17,
18, 11, 13, 20, 25, 18, 15, 19, 21, 21, 7, 12, 23, 31, 16, 19,
23, 15, 25, 19, 15, 25, 25, 16, 29, 15, 26, 29, 23, 24, 20, 19,
14, 27, 22, 26)
Fun1(x)
mean std
19.800000 5.256677
```

4. If the value of the sym variable is 2, then the corresponding output will be as follows:

```
sym <- 2
Fun2 <- switch(sym, function(x) c(mean=mean(x), std=sd(x)),
function(x), c(med=median(x), mad=mad(x)))
Fun2(x)
med       mad
19.0000 5.9304
```

How it works...

The switch function takes an integer value input as statement and then returns an item from the list based on the value of the input statement. In the example implemented in this recipe, the list contains two elements. The two elements are two functions to calculate the summary statistics of a given numeric variables. The switch(statement, list) statement takes the input through the sym variable. If the value of sym is 1, then the switch function will return the first element from the item list, and it will return the second element if the value of sym is 2.

Since the item in the list is a function, to calculate actual summary statistics, you have to call the resultant function as it has been done.

There's more...

There might be a situation where you end up having a value of `sym` that is beyond the number of items in the list. For example, it could be `sym=3` or `sym=0`. If this happens, then the `switch` function will return `NULL`.

Comparing the performance of switch and series of the if...else statements

Sometimes, you are in a situation where you will execute one task from a list of alternatives based on a conditional value of another variable. In this case, you have two ways of doing it, either using the `switch` function or a series of the `if...else if...else` statement. The question is which one performs better. In this recipe, you will assess the performance of these two alternatives.

Getting ready

You are given a vector of numeric values representing the number of hours spent on social media in a week as follows:

```
13, 21, 19, 18, 21, 16, 21, 24, 17, 18, 12, 18, 29, 17, 18, 11, 13,
20, 25, 18, 15, 19, 21, 21, 7, 12, 23, 31, 16, 19, 23, 15, 25, 19,
15, 25, 25, 16, 29, 15, 26, 29, 23, 24, 20, 19, 14, 27, 22, 26
```

The task is to calculate the mean, standard deviation, median, and MAD based on a value of another variable `sym`. If the value of the `sym` variable is `classical`, then you will calculate the mean and standard deviation. Alternatively if the value of `sym` is `robust`, then you will calculate the median and MAD. Also, you will implement this task using the `switch` function and `if...else if...else`. Once you have done the implementation, you will repeat the calculation a certain number of times, say 100,000 times, and then calculate the total time required.

How to do it...

Let's take a look at the following steps to perform the given task of calculating the mean, standard deviation, median, and MAD based on a value of another variable `sym`:

1. Execute the first implementation using the `switch` function as follows:

```
option1 <- function(x, sym){
  switch(sym, classical = c(mean= mean(x, na.rm = T), std =
  sd(x, na.rm = T)), robust = c(med = median(x, na.rm = T),
  mad = mad(x, na.rm = T))
  )
}
```

2. Execute the second implementation using the `if...else if ...else` statement as follows:

```
option2 <- function(x, sym){
  if(sym=="classical"){
    out <- c(mean = mean(x,na.rm = T), std= sd(x,na.rm = T))
    return(out)
  }
  else if(sym=="robust"){
    out <- c(med = median(x, na.rm = T), mad = mad(x, na.rm =
    T))
    return(out)
  }
  else return(NULL)
}
```

3. Now, to calculate the performance of these two options, you will use the given variable as input and repeat the same calculation over 100,000 times using the `microbenchmark()` function from the `microbenchmark` library in R as follows:</li>

```
inputVec <- c(13, 21, 19, 18, 21, 16, 21, 24, 17, 18, 12, 18,
29, 17, 18, 11, 13, 20, 25, 18, 15, 19, 21, 21, 7, 12, 23, 31,
16, 19, 23, 15, 25, 19, 15, 25, 25, 16, 29, 15, 26, 29, 23, 24,
20, 19, 14, 27, 22, 26)

library(microbenchmark)

microbenchmark(option1(x,"classical"), option2(x,"classical"),
times = 100000)
Unit: microseconds
  expr                          min    lq    mean    median  uq
```

```
option1(x,"classical")  19.819 22.298 27.76835   23.713 26.898
option2(x, "classical") 21.589 24.420 31.27799   25.836 29.022

max         neval  cld
4073.834    1e+05    a
93406.523 1e+05    b


microbenchmark(option1(x,"robust"), option2(x,"robust"),
times = 100000)

Unit: microseconds
expr                     min      lq       mean    median   uq
option1(x, "robust")  61.934  71.136  90.09696  74.322 105.819
option2(x, "robust")  64.058  73.260  90.23864  76.799 109.004


uq          max       neval  cld
105.819     137634.38 1e+05    a
109.004     12657.86  1e+05    a
```

How it works...

The first step is to write both functions, one using `switch` and another using the `if...else if...else` statement. Once the function writing part is completed, you can calculate the elapsed time of a certain operation. To see the calculation time, use the `microbenchmark()` library in R. The `microbenchmark()` function takes two alternative functions as input and also another input telling the function how many times the repetition should be done. The output of the `microbenchmark()` function is in microseconds. The output essentially shows that the `switch` option takes less time than `if...else if...else`.

Using for loop for iterations

The most convenient way to perform iterative operation in R is the use of a `for` loop. Suppose you are given a dataset with five variables representing five different diseases for 10 people. All your variables are binary. Your task is to calculate the frequency of each variable as well as the cross-frequency of all pair-wise variables. Using a `for` loop, you can easily complete this task. In this recipe, you will implement a `for` loop to calculate the disease frequency and the frequency of all pair-wise variables.

Getting ready

Let's consider you are given the following dataset `mat`:

```
set.seed(1234)
mat<-matrix(sample(c(0,1),50,replace = T),nrow = 10,ncol=5)
rownames(mat) <- paste("patient", paste(1:10),sep="")
colnames(mat) <- c("diabetes", "hypertension", "asthma",
"jointPain", "fever")
> mat
          diabetes hypertension asthma jointPain fever
patient1         0            1      0         0     1
patient2         1            1      0         0     1
patient3         1            0      0         0     0
patient4         1            1      0         1     1
patient5         1            0      0         0     0
patient6         1            1      1         1     1
patient7         0            0      1         0     1
patient8         0            0      1         0     0
patient9         1            0      1         1     0
patient10        1            0      0         1     1
```

The task is to calculate the frequency of each disease and all pair-wise diseases, for example, `diabetes` and `hypertension` or `diabetes` and `asthma`.

How to do it...

There will be total 10 possible pair-wise combinations of variables and five individual variables. You have to calculate a total 15 frequencies. To get all possible combinations of the variables, you will need to use the `for` loop two times, also known as **nested** loop. The code is as follows:

```
out<-matrix(NA, nrow = ncol(mat), ncol = ncol(mat))
  for(i in 1:ncol(mat)){
    for(j in 1:ncol(mat)){
      colI <- mat[,i]
      colJ <- mat[,j]
      out[i,j] <- t(colI) %*% colJ
    }
  }
```

The preceding code snippet will give you the following output:

```
> out
     [,1] [,2] [,3] [,4] [,5]
[1,]   7    3    2    4    4
[2,]   3    4    1    2    4
[3,]   2    1    4    2    2
[4,]   4    2    2    4    3
[5,]   4    4    2    3    6
```

How it works...

The `set.seed()` function has been used to make the example reproducible. The matrix `mat` contains five columns and 10 rows representing the binary variable of each disease. The `rownames()` and `colnames()` functions have been used to give the name of the rows and columns for easy understanding.

Initially, the output matrix `out` is created with all `NA` values. The number of columns of the `out` matrix will be the total number of columns in the original input matrix, and the number of rows of the `out` matrix will be the same as the number of columns of the original input matrix.

To get all possible combinations, the first loop runs from one to a number of columns and the second loop also runs from one to a number of columns. These two loops together give all possible combinations of the variables. The following two lines have been used to get the appropriate columns for the calculation:

```
colI <- mat[,i]
colJ <- mat[,j]
```

After getting the two columns, the matrix multiplication of transposing the first column with the second column gives the required result. If the value of the columns i and j are the same, then it will give the frequency of the ith variable. However, if the value of i and j is different, then it will give the cross-frequency.

Vectorised operation versus for loop

One of the well-known drawbacks in R is use of the `for` loop. This is relatively very slow compared to other software. However, if you have avoided the use of loop while doing the same task using the matrix operation, then it is a lot faster. In this recipe, you will compare a vectorized version with a `for` loop to do the same task.

Getting ready

Consider a situation where you have a dataset with 500 columns representing 500 binary variables of a certain characteristic. In the dataset, you have a total of 900 observations. The objective is to calculate the frequency of 1's in each of the 500 variables and all the possible pair-wise combinations of the variables. The dataset is given in the CSV file, so to implement this recipe, you will need to read the dataset from the CSV file and then convert it into a matrix as follows:

```
bigBinaryData <- read.csv("loopVectorization.csv")
binMat <- as.matrix(bigBinaryData) # to convert data frame into a
matrix
```

How to do it...

Write a function using a `for` loop to execute the targeted operation. Also, write another function without using a loop. Let's take a look at the following steps and see how we can do the preceding two tasks:

1. Execute the following code snippet that depicts a function using a loop:

```
loopOperation <- function(mat){
  out<-matrix(NA, nrow = ncol(mat), ncol = ncol(mat))
  for(i in 1:ncol(mat)){
    for(j in 1:ncol(mat)){
      colI <- mat[,i]
      colJ <- mat[,j]
      out[i,j] <- t(colI) %*% colJ
    }
  }
  return(out)
}
```

2. Execute another function without using the loop, but use only the matrix operation as shown in the following code snippet:

```
vectorizedOp <- function(mat){
  return(t(mat) %*% mat)
}

library(microbenchmark) # To compare performance of the functions
microbenchmark(loopOperation(mat = binMat), vectorizedOp(mat = binMat))
        Unit: milliseconds
    expr                          min         lq          mean
```

```
vectorized(mat=binMat)       7.009144    9.30052    10.67089
loopOperation(mat=binMat) 6826.260664 7476.98113 7766.50789

 median        uq        max       neval cld
 9.89367      11.8099    21.3325    100   a
 7650.74206   8115.6440  9333.9608  100   b
```

How it works...

Since the dataset was in a CSV file, after reading it into the R environment, it got stored as a data frame. In this recipe, you will use the matrix operation, so you need to convert the data frame into a matrix. That's why, in the *Getting ready* section, the data frame has been converted into a matrix using the `as.matrix()` function.

In the next step, two functions were written, one using a `for` loop to calculate the frequency of each column in the dataset and also all possible pair-wise frequencies, and the other function also did the same task but it was implemented without using any loop. The second function uses a certain logic to calculate the frequency and cross-frequency, that is, if all of the variables in a dataset are binary, then if you multiply the transpose of the data matrix with the data matrix itself, it will give the desired results.

5
R Objects and Classes

In this chapter, you will learn how to create the S3 and S4 objects and how to use them in a variety of applications. Specifically, you will orient yourself using the following recipes:

- Defining a new S3 class
- Defining methods for the S3 class
- Creating a generic function and defining a method for the S3 class
- Defining a new S4 class
- Defining methods for an S4 class
- Creating a function to return an object of the S4 class

Introduction

In the development of a computer program (software design), the process of defining data types of a data structure along with the types of operations using user-defined functions on the data structure is known as **object-oriented programming (OOP)**. In the OOP process, the data structure becomes an object, and the function and the data itself are contained within that object. The R programming has a system of OOP using generic functions. The two most popular classes are used in R to do OOP, namely, S3 and S4. In this chapter, you will learn about both S3 and S4 classes and then create new methods based on those classes.

Defining a new S3 class

In OOP, the class and method play an important role. The behavior of a generic function depends on the class and the methods dispatched on it. In this recipe, you will create a new S3 class for an object in R.

Getting ready

The S3 class is the most popular class in R. Primarily, the majority of R objects come with default S3 classes. There is no rigid definition of S3 classes in R. Rather it is simple and intuitive to use. In this recipe, you will create a new S3 class, say robustSummary, for a numeric vector. Let's say you have a numeric vector of the default class numeric, but your objective is to create a new class robustSummary and attach it to the object.

Here is the given numeric object with 50 items representing the number of hours spent on social media in a week:

```
x <- c(13, 21, 19, 18, 21, 16, 21, 24, 17, 18, 12, 18, 29, 17, 18,
11, 13, 20, 25, 18, 15, 19, 21, 21, 7, 12, 23, 31, 16, 19, 23, 15,
25, 19, 15, 25, 25, 16, 29, 15, 26, 29, 23, 24, 20, 19, 14, 27, 22, 26)
```

How to do it...

Let's take a look at the following steps to create a new S3 class for an object in R:

1. Now you are given the object of default class. So, before creating new class, it is good to check the name of default class of the object. To check the class of any R object, the code is class(objectName) as follows:

```
class(x)
[1] "numeric"
```

2. To create the new class, class() will be used as class(nameofobject) <- "classname" as follows:

```
class(x) <- "robustSummary"
class(x)
[1] "robustSummary"
```

3. The creation of an S3 object is pretty informal. The user can define the class according to their needs and wishes. To remove the class from an object, you can use the unclass(objectname) function. However, it will only remove the user-defined class and then return to the default class. For example, if you remove the class from object x, then it will again show the default "numeric" class, as shown in the following code snippet:

```
y <- unclass(x)
class(y)
[1] "numeric"
```

How it works...

The `class()` function works in a manner similar to the `assign()` function. It takes an object name as input and then assigns a character value as the class name. The same function can be used to assign and remove class names. Interestingly, you can remove only the user-defined class name, but the object will always show its default class after removing the user-defined one. In the preceding example in the previous section, the line `class(x)` returns the default class of the object and the output was `"numeric"`. The same function has been used to assign the new class `robustSummary`.

After assigning the new class name, the `unclass()` function actually removes the newly class name from the object and assigns it to the default `numeric` class.

There's more...

Once you have created a new class for an object in R, you might think what is the use of the class? The answer is simple: you can utilize the class name to define a new generic function to perform a customized task. For example, you can define a generic function based on the class `"robustSummary"`, and the new function will only give you the robust descriptive statistics such as median, MAD, and quartiles.

You can also use any conditional operation based on the condition satisfying the class name as follows:

```
if(class(x)=="robustSummary") print("A new class has been defined")
```

See also

In the next recipe, you will learn how to use class names to define a new method of a generic function.

Defining methods for the S3 class

A method is just an implementation of a generic function of any R object with a particular class of interest. The method in any OOP is the efficient way to perform certain customized tasks. Once you have a class and associated method, then you just need to call the generic function and the method. The method actually does not perform any operation, rather it just dispatches a specific function based on the class of the objects. For example, when you call `print()` on a `data.frame` object, it calls `print.data.frame()`. In this recipe, you will define a new method for the newly defined class `robustSummary` so that it only shows robust descriptive statistics of an object.

Getting ready

In R, generally if you write the object name into the console, then it automatically prints its internal elements. For example, take a look at the following code snippet:

```
x <- c(13, 21, 19, 18, 21, 16, 21, 24, 17, 18, 12, 18, 29, 17, 18,
11, 13, 20, 25, 18, 15, 19, 21, 21, 7, 12, 23, 31, 16, 19, 23, 15,
25, 19, 15, 25, 25, 16, 29, 15, 26, 29, 23, 24, 20, 19, 14, 27, 22,
26)

class(x) <- "robustSummary"
```

Now, if you just type x in the R console, it will print all the items in the object x and its class name. In R, when you call an object into the R console, it actually looks for a method for the class of the given object. If there is no method available for that class, then it automatically calls `print.default()` and produces the output accordingly. In this example, calling the function `print()` is equivalent to calling `print.default()`, as shown in the following code:

```
> print(x)
[1]  13 21 19 18 21 16 21 24 17 18 12 18 29 17 18 11 13 20 25 18 15
19 21 21  7 12 23 31 16
[30] 19 23 15 25 19 15 25 25 16 29 15 26 29 23 24 20 19 14 27 22 26
attr(,"class")
[1] "robustSummary"

> print.default(x)
[1]  13 21 19 18 21 16 21 24 17 18 12 18 29 17 18 11 13 20 25 18 15
19 21 21  7 12 23 31 16
[30] 19 23 15 25 19 15 25 25 16 29 15 26 29 23 24 20 19 14 27 22 26
attr(,"class")
[1] "robustSummary"
```

However, if you call it using the class name, then you will get the following error:

```
print.robustSummary(x)
  Error: could not find function "print.robustSummary"
```

The error states that there is no function or method for the class robustSummary. In this recipe, you will define a method for the generic function print() for the object class robustSummary.

How to do it...

Let's take a look at the following steps to define a method for the generic function print() with the robustSummary class:

1. You now have the object with the class robustSummary. Now, the task is to define a method for the generic function print() with this class so that it will act like print.robustSummary(). The function can be written as follows:

```
print.robustSummary <- function(obj){
    cat("Median ", median(obj), "\n")
    cat("Median Absolute Deviation (MAD)", mad(obj), "\n")
    cat("First Quartile (Q1)", as.numeric(quantile(obj, probs =
    0.25)), "\n")
    cat("Third Quartile (Q3)", as.numeric(quantile(obj, probs =
    0.75)))
}
```

2. Once the function writing is complete, you can simply call the object into the R console. It will then automatically print the desired output provided that the class of the object is robustSummary. For example, take a look at the following code snippet:

```
> x
Median   19
Median Absolute Deviation (MAD) 5.9304
First Quartile (Q1) 16
Third Quartile (Q3) 23.75
```

3. You can also call it using `print.robustSummary(x)`, as shown in the following code snippet:

```
> print.robustSummary(x)
Median   19
Median Absolute Deviation (MAD) 5.9304
First Quartile (Q1) 16
Third Quartile (Q3) 23.75
```

4. Moreover, you can also call it by only calling the `print()` function, as follows:

```
> print(x)
Median   19
Median Absolute Deviation (MAD) 5.9304
First Quartile (Q1) 16
Third Quartile (Q3) 23.75
```

How it works...

The print part is a generic function in R. A generic function is a generalized concept, for example, printing results is a generic concept and the corresponding generic function is print. This function works differently based on the class of the objects. The object x here has the class `robustSummary`. As a result, whenever you call the object itself into the R console, it actually calls the `print.robustSummary()` function.

However, before calling the `print.robustSummary()` function, you must define it and specify the behavior of the function; for example, it should know what to print, what should be the format, and so on.

There's more...

As discussed, the method works based on generic concepts and the class names. If the class name changed, then the behavior of the corresponding function will also change based on it. For example, if you remove the "`robustSummary`" class from the object x then the `print()` function will work differently:

```
> y <- unclass(x)
> y
[1] 13 21 19 18 21 16 21 24 17 18 12 18 29 17 18 11 13 20 25 18
15 19 21 21  7 12 23 31 16
[30] 19 23 15 25 19 15 25 25 16 29 15 26 29 23 24 20 19 14 27
22 26
```

```
> class(y) <- "robustSummary"
> y
Median  19
Median Absolute Deviation (MAD) 5.9304
First Quartile (Q1) 16
Third Quartile (Q3) 23.75
```

In the first block of code and output, the class x has been removed and assigned the new object into y. Then the generic function `print()` has been called. The output is just the internal elements printed into the console.

However, later on, when the `robustSummary` class has been assigned into the object y, then the `print()` function behaves differently. This is the beauty of OOP.

See also

Though the S3 class is informal in nature, the definition is easy and intuitive. To learn more about classes and methods, follow the later recipes, *Defining a new S4 class* and *Defining methods for an S4 class*.

Creating a generic function and defining a method for the S3 class

A generic function is an encapsulation of any generic concept such as printing, calculating summary information of any R objects, creating graphs, and so on. The generic function does not perform any calculation, rather it just dispatches methods based on the class of the objects. In this recipe, you will create your own generic function and then define the method for the class `robustStatistics`.

Getting ready

Suppose you want to create a generic function alternative to `summary()` in R. The name of the function is `robSum()`. The default action will be just to check the class and produce a message whether the input object has a certain class or not. In the second stage, you will define a method for the new generic function.

How to do it...

Let's take a look at the following steps:

1. The new generic function can be created as follows:

```
robSum <- function(obj) {
  UseMethod("robSum")
}
```

2. A default method for `robSum()` is created as follows:

```
robSum.default <- function(obj){
  cat("This is a generic function for the object class
  'robustSummary'")
}
```

3. A new method for the `robSum()` generic function for the object class can be created as follows:

```
# robustSummary
robSum.robustSummary <- function(obj){
  cat("Median ", median(obj), "\n")
  cat("Median Absolute Deviation (MAD)", mad(obj), "\n")
  cat("First Quartile (Q1)", as.numeric(quantile(obj, probs =
  0.25)), "\n")
  cat("Third Quartile (Q3)", as.numeric(quantile(obj, probs =
  0.75)))
}
```

How it works...

The first phase of defining a generic function is defining a function and mentioning the use method for that function. The function `robSum()` has use method `robSum`; in other words, using this name, you have to call this generic function.

Every generic function usually has a default method where the default task has been defined. In this example, the default method is just printing a line of text `This is a generic function for the object class robustSummary`. Whenever the default method of this `robSum()` generic function call or the input object's class is not `robustSummary`, it will print this default line.

The final step is to define the method for the targeted class. In this example, the class name is `robustSummary`. The method has been defined by the `robSum.robustSummary()` function. Whenever the input object has the class `robustSummary`, it will print the median, MAD, first quartile, and third quartile. This function will act like an alternative generic implementation of the `print()` function with the `robustSummary` method.

Now, let's create an object with the `"robustSummary"` class and call the newly created generic function and methods, as shown in the following code:

```
> set.seed(123)  # to make the result reproducible
> newX <- rnorm(50) # generating 50 ranodm numbers from standard
normal distribution
> robSum.default(obj = newX)
This is a generic function for the object class 'robustSummary'

> class(newX) <- "robustSummary"
> robSum.default(obj = newX)
This is a generic function for the object class 'robustSummary'

> robSum.robustSummary(obj = newX)
Median   -0.07264039
Median Absolute Deviation (MAD) 0.9164537
First Quartile (Q1) -0.559317
Third Quartile (Q3) 0.698177
```

There's more...

The function name is usually the name of the object that has been assigned while creating the function itself as follows:

```
myFun <- function(obj){...}
```

Here, the name of function is `myFun`. Now, create the function and define a use method as follows:

```
myFun <- function(obj){UseMethod("robSum")}
```

In this case, the function can be called using the name `robSum`. This way, you can hide the original code of the function.

Defining a new S4 class

You have seen that the S3 class does not have any formal definition, and as a result, there is a greater chance of making naïve mistakes. The S4 class is more rigorous, and it has a formal definition and a uniform way to create objects. In this recipe, you will define a new S4 class robustSummary.

Getting ready

Suppose you have a numeric vector x representing the number of hours spent on social media in a week. You want to define a new S4 class that will display the robust descriptive statistics. The name of the new class will be robustSummary, and the individual items of this class will be as follows:

- Median
- MAD
- First quartile
- Third quartile

Here is the original vector with 50 numeric values:

```
x <- c(13, 21, 19, 18, 21, 16, 21, 24, 17, 18, 12, 18, 29, 17, 18,
11, 13, 20, 25, 18, 15, 19, 21, 21, 7, 12, 23, 31, 16, 19, 23, 15,
25, 19, 15, 25, 25, 16, 29, 15, 26, 29, 23, 24, 20, 19, 14, 27, 22,
26)
```

How to do it...

Take a look at the following steps:

1. To define a new S4 class, the following two functions have been used:
   - new()
   - setClass()

2. The objective is to calculate the robust descriptive summary statistics and then store the result in a new object with the S4 class. Here is the function to calculate the robust summary statistics:

```
robSum <- function(obj){
  med <- median(obj)
  mad <- mad(obj)
  q1 <- as.numeric(quantile(obj, probs = 0.25))
  q3 <- as.numeric(quantile(obj, probs = 0.75))
  return(list(median=med, mad=mad, q1= q1, q3=q3))
}
```

3. This function will return a list of objects with the calculated robust summary statistics. Now, the task is to define an S4 class with the following result:

```
rStats <- robSum(obj=x)
rStatsS4 <- new("robustSummary", median=rStats$median,
mad=rStats$mad, q1=rStats$q1, q3=rStats$q3)
```

How it works...

The `new()` function is specially designed to define a new S4 class. In this recipe, the function `robSum()` is not a mandatory part of defining the S4 class, but this function has been used to calculate the summary statistics, and then, the output of this function has been encapsulated into the S4 class.

The `robSum()` function is an R function to calculate robust descriptive statistics. Then, the output of this function has been passed through the `new()` function to define the new S4 class `robustSummary`. The question is how do we check whether the object created using the `new()` function is an S4 object?

To check whether `rStatsS4` is an object of class S4, you need to use the following code:

```
> isS4(rStatsS4)
[1] TRUE
```

The output of the new S4 object will be as follows:

```
> rStatsS4
An object of class "robustSummary"
Slot "median":
[1] 19
Slot "mad":
[1] 5.9304
Slot "q1":
[1] 16
Slot "q3":
[1] 23.75
```

There's more...

Though you can directly use the new() function to define a new S4 class, there is another more generalized way to define a new S4 class using a constructor function as follows:

```
> robustSummary <- setClass("robustSummary",
slots=list(median="numeric", mad="numeric",
q1="numeric", q3="numeric"))

> robustSummary
class generator function for class "robustSummary" from package
'.GlobalEnv'
function (...)
new("robustSummary", ...)
```

See also

To get detailed discussion on the S4 class, follow https://cran.r-project.org/doc/contrib/Genolini-S4tutorialV0-5en.pdf.

Defining methods for an S4 class

Like S3 classes, generic functions, and methods, there are similar things also available in the S4 object class. In this recipe, you will create a new method for a generic function for an S4 object class.

Getting ready

To define a new method for an S4 class of object, first you need an object of class S4. Here is the code to create an object of S4 class robustSummary2:

```
x <- c(13, 21, 19, 18, 21, 16, 21, 24, 17, 18, 12, 18, 29, 17, 18,
11, 13, 20, 25, 18, 15, 19, 21, 21, 7, 12, 23, 31, 16, 19, 23,
15, 25, 19, 15, 25, 25, 16, 29, 15, 26, 29, 23, 24, 20, 19,
14, 27, 22, 26)
robSum <- function(obj){
  med <- median(obj)
  mad <- mad(obj)
  q1 <- as.numeric(quantile(obj, probs = 0.25))
  q3 <- as.numeric(quantile(obj, probs = 0.75))
  return(list(median=med, mad=mad, q1= q1, q3=q3))
}

rStats <- robSum(obj=x)
rStatsS4 <- new("robustSummary", median=rStats$median,
mad=rStats$mad, q1=rStats$q1, q3=rStats$q3)

> isS4(rStatsS4)
[1] TRUE
```

Now, you have an object rStatsS4 of class S4. The task is to create a new method for this class to display the output in a customized structure.

How to do it...

The S4 object class has a generic function equivalent to the print() generic function for the S3 class of objects. The function "show" is a generic function that works similarly to the print() function in the S3 system. You will write a method for the "show" function for the "robustSummary" S4 class as follows:

```
setMethod("show",
          "robustSummary",
          function(object) {
            cat("The median is ",object@median, " with median
            absolute deviation (MAD) = ", object@mad, "\n")
            cat("First and Third Quartile is", object@q1, "and",
            object@q3)
          }
)
```

How it works...

The newly created S4 object `rStatsS4` displays the results into the R console as follows:

```
> rStatsS4
An object of class "robustSummary"
Slot "median":
[1] 19
Slot "mad":
 [1] 5.9304
Slot "q1":
 [1] 16
Slot "q3":
 [1] 23.75
```

This is the default method of the `show()` generic function. Once you have defined the method for the class `robustSummary`, the result will display as you defined within the method. Here is the result using the newly defined method for the `robustSummary` class:

```
> show(rStatsS4)
The median is  19  with median absolute deviation (MAD) =  5.9304
First and Third Quartile is 16 and 23.75

> rStatsS4
The median is  19  with median absolute deviation (MAD) =  5.9304
First and Third Quartile is 16 and 23.75
```

There's more...

Since an S4 class has a more rigorous structure, you can set validation rules for the class that you are creating and using. The `setValidation()` function is the function to set rules for validation. For example, each of the slots of the `robustSummary` S4 class has numeric values. However, if you mistakenly enter a "character" value, then it will give you a default error message. To handle this type of situation, you could use `setValidation()`. For more details, follow the document mentioned into the next section.

See also

To get details on the S4 class, go to `https://cran.r-project.org/doc/contrib/Genolini-S4tutorialV0-5en.pdf`.

 You can access elements of S3 objects using the `$` sign. This is very similar to accessing columns from a data frame. However, to get access to individual items from an S4 class object, you must use the `@` sign, for example, `object@slot1`.

Creating a function to return an object of the S4 class

In R, whenever you write a function, by default the return object gets an S3 class but if you want to return an object that has S4 class, then you should explicitly define the class within the body of the function. In the previous recipes, you saw that the class has been defined outside of the function body. In this recipe, you will write a function that will return an object of the S4 class.

Getting ready

Your objective is to create a function that will calculate the following two types of descriptive statistics:

- Classical (mean and standard deviation)
- Robust (median and MAD)

The following is the vector of numeric values for the input. Your new function will take two inputs, one is the numeric vector and another is the type (either `"classical"` or `"robust"`). The function will return an object of the S4 class containing the following results:

```
x <- c(13, 21, 19, 18, 21, 16, 21, 24, 17, 18, 12, 18, 29, 17, 18,
11, 13, 20, 25, 18, 15, 19, 21, 21, 7, 12, 23, 31, 16, 19, 23, 15,
25, 19, 15, 25, 25, 16, 29, 15, 26, 29, 23, 24, 20, 19, 14, 27, 22,
26)
```

How to do it...

Let's give a name to the function that you are going to write here, desStat, and define its action as follows:

```
desStat <- function(numVec, type="classical"){
  if(!is.numeric(numVec))
    stop("The input must be numeric")
  average <- mean(numVec, na.rm = T)
  std <- sd(numVec, na.rm = T)
  med <- median(numVec, na.rm = T)
  mad <- mad(numVec, na.rm = T)
  descriptiveStats <- setClass("descriptiveStats",
  slots=list(centre="numeric",
  spread="numeric"))
  if(type=="classical")
    return(new("descriptiveStats", centre=average, spread=std))
    if(type=="robust")
        return(new("descriptiveStats", centre=med, spread=mad))
  }

desStat(x)
An object of class "descriptiveStats"
Slot "centre":
[1] 19.8

Slot "spread":
[1] 5.256677
```

How it works...

This function has an input validation step. If the input vector is not numeric, then it will give a message as "The input must be numeric". The validation part has been defined as follows:

```
if(!is.numeric(numVec))
    stop("The input must be numeric")
```

Once the validation step passes, the function internally calculates everything for summary statistics, such as mean, standard deviation, median, and MAD. In the next step, the S4 class definition has been introduced as follows:

```
descriptiveStats <- setClass("descriptiveStats",
slots=list(centre="numeric", spread="numeric"))
```

Now, based on the value of the `type` argument in the function, it returns either classical or robust descriptive statistics and the return object will have the S4 class `descriptiveStats`.

There's more...

Like the input validation, you can set the validation for the class as well using `setValidation()` while defining the class properties.

See also

To get details on the S4 class, visit `https://cran.r-project.org/doc/contrib/Genolini-S4tutorialV0-5en.pdf`.

6
Querying, Filtering, and Summarizing

In this chapter, you will explore the dplyr library for data processing. This is one of the most popular libraries in R for data processing. This chapter covers the following recipes:

- Using the pipe operator for data processing
- Efficient and fast summarization using the dplyr verbs
- Using the customized function within the dplyr verbs
- Using the select verb for data processing
- Using the filter verb for data processing
- Using the arrange verb for data processing
- Using mutate for data processing
- Using summarise to summarize dataset

Introduction

Preparing dataset for statistical analysis is one of the most important steps in any data analytical domain. Data pre-processing takes almost 80 percent of the total data analysis task. There are lots of different libraries developed over time for data pre-processing, but `dplyr` is one of the most popular and memory-efficient data-processing libraries. In this chapter, you will use the functionalities within the `dplyr` library to do some pre-processing. The USA domestic airlines data has been downloaded from the website of the Bureau of Transportation Statistics (`https://www.transtats.bts.gov`). This dataset will be used throughout the chapter.

The dataset contains 61 variables rating time period, airline, origin, destination, departure performance, arrival performance, cancellations and diversions, flight summaries, and causes of delay. Due to the huge size of the data, only the year 2016 has been considered. You will be redirected to the official website (`https://www.transtats.bts.gov`) for full details of the variables.

Using the pipe operator for data processing

Whenever we work in any data analysis projects, we usually filter, summarize by groups, and then create plots out of that. In this task sequence, the output of one task is usually the input of another task and then move forward. The most naïve practice is to create temporary objects by taking the output of each step and using that object as an input for later stage. This approach takes lots of memory, and usually, the whole operation is time consuming. In this recipe, you will use a specialized operator, known as the pipe operator, to do the sequential tasks. Though this operator is implemented in the `magrittr` library, it is mostly used in combination with the `dplyr` functions.

Getting ready

To use the pipe operator in association with the `dplyr` functionalities, you need to install the following libraries:

- `magrittr`
- `dplyr`

During installation of these two libraries, make sure that you also install the necessary dependencies. Here is the code to install the preceding two libraries:

```
install.packages(c("magrittr", "dplyr"), dependencies = T)
```

To learn more about installing R libraries, see the *Installing R libraries from various sources* recipe, in `Chapter 1`, *Installing and Configuring R and its Libraries*.

The dataset for this recipe is the USA domestic airline data. The objective is to summarize the delay time by each month and then visualize the results. Here are the specific variables of interest in this recipe:

- Month
- Departure delay

In the original dataset, the departure delay might contain some negative values indicating early departure. First, you have to drop those negative numbers.

How to do it...

The sequence of tasks will be as follows:

1. Import the dataset.
2. Carry out variables selection by taking only relevant variables.
3. Remove the rows with negative values in departure delay.
4. Calculate mean delay over months.
5. Visualize the results.

Here is the code that performs these operations in one go:

```
USAairlineData2016 <- read.csv("USAairlineData2016.csv", as.is
= T)
USAairlineData2016 %>%
  select(MONTH, DEP_DELAY) %>%
  filter(DEP_DELAY>=0) %>%
  group_by(MONTH) %>%
  summarize(avgDelay=mean(DEP_DELAY)) %>%
  qplot(factor(MONTH),avgDelay,data=.,group=1,geom=c("line",
  "point")) %>%
  add(xlab("Month")) %>%
  add(ylab("Mean delay (in min)")) %>%
  add(ggtitle("Mean delay in departure over months of 2016"))
  %>%
  add(theme_bw()) %>%
  print
```

How it works...

After importing the data into the R environment, the code works as follows:

1. It takes the entire dataset as an input in the first place. It will work as the input for the function `select()`.
2. Within the `select()` function, it only keeps the variables of month and departure delay.
3. The `filter()` function takes the output from the `select()` function and drops those rows that have negative values in the `DEP_DELAY` variable.

4. The `group_by` function instructs the `summarize()` function that the calculation should be grouped by the variable specified into the `group_by` section.

5. The `summarize()` function then calculates the mean departure delay for each month and supplies the output data to the plotting function `qplot()`.

6. The `qplot()` function produces a line plot of mean delay of departure for each month, and then, the `add()` function performs some formatting types of task, such as adding axis title and plot title, and finally, it applies the black-and-white theme.

7. The `print()` function, finally, produces the output into the R plotting device as follows:

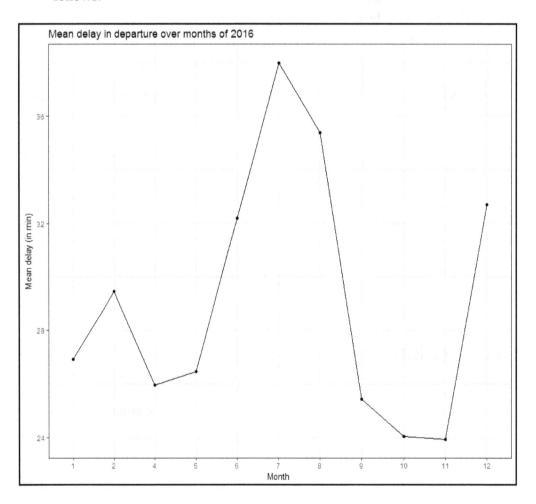

There's more...

In this example, the forward pipe operator has been used. You should be careful when using any function within the sequence. If any function does not accept `data=.` as an argument, then you might get an error. The `data=.` argument is actually taking the dataset as input from the output of previous steps.

See also

There are other pipe operators available, such as compound operator `%<>%` and `%$%`. To get complete exposure to the pipe operator, you will be redirected to the documentation of the `magrittr` library from CRAN.

Efficient and fast summarization using the dplyr verbs

In R, there are many ways to do data summarization, but when the dataset gets bigger, some of the base functions take a longer time to complete the task. The `dplyr` library is designed to handle a larger dataset to perform this kind of task efficiently, and faster than the default base R functionality. In this recipe, you will explore the speed of the `dplyr` verb to calculate summary statistics from a large dataset and compare the elapsed time with that of the base R functionality.

Getting ready

The dataset for this recipe is the USA domestic airline 2016 data, which has been downloaded from the bureau of transportation statistics (`https://www.transtat.bts.gov`). In this recipe, the objective is to calculate four number summary statistics (minimum, mean, median, and maximum) of departure delay for each month and for each origin of flight. The variables of interest in this recipe are as follows:

- Month
- Origin
- Departure delay

The summary statistics will be calculated using the base R functionality and using `dplyr` to compare the processing times.

How to do it...

Here are the steps involved in this recipe:

1. Import the dataset into the R environment.
2. Calculate the summary statistics using the `dplyr` library.
3. Calculate the summary statistics using the base R functionality such as aggregate.
4. Calculate the performance of *step 2* and *step 3* in terms of elapsed time using the `microbenchmark` library.

   The following code block contains implementation of *step 1* and *step 2*:

   ```
   USAairlineData2016 <- read.csv("USAairlineData2016.csv", as.is
   = T)

   desStat <- USAairlineData2016 %>%
     select(MONTH, ORIGIN, DEP_DELAY) %>%
     group_by(ORIGIN, MONTH) %>%
     summarize(
       MIN_DELAY = min(DEP_DELAY, na.rm=T),
       MEAN_DELAY = mean(DEP_DELAY, na.rm=T),
       MEDIAN_DELAY = median(DEP_DELAY, na.rm=T),
       MAX_DELAY = max(DEP_DELAY, na.rm=T)
     )
   ```

5. To implement *step 3*, first, you need a new function to use within the aggregate function. The new function `fourNumSum` has been implemented in the following code block and then passes this new function into the aggregate function to calculate summary statistics:

   ```
   fourNumSum <- function(x){
     MIN_DELAY = min(x, na.rm=T)
     MEAN_DELAY = mean(x, na.rm=T)
     MEDIAN_DELAY = median(x, na.rm=T)
     MAX_DELAY = max(x, na.rm=T)
     return(c(MIN_DELAY=MIN_DELAY,MEAN_DELAY=MEAN_DELAY,
     MEDIAN_DELAY=MEDIAN_DELAY,MAX_DELAY=MAX_DELAY))
   }

   desStat2 <- with(USAairlineData2016, aggregate(DEP_DELAY,
   list(ORIGIN,MONTH), fourNumSum))
   ```

6. In *step 4*, to calculate the elapsed time by both approaches implemented in *step 2* and *step 3*, you need two separate functions that perform the same task as *step 2* and *step 3*.

7. After defining the new function, you will then call the `microbenchmark()` function from the `microbenchmark` library to calculate the time elapsed by both approaches:

```
funDPLYR <- function(data){
  desStat <- data %>%
    select(MONTH, ORIGIN, DEP_DELAY) %>%
    group_by(ORIGIN, MONTH) %>%
    summarize(
      MIN_DELAY = min(DEP_DELAY, na.rm=T),
      MEAN_DELAY = mean(DEP_DELAY, na.rm=T),
      MEDIAN_DELAY = median(DEP_DELAY, na.rm=T),
      MAX_DELAY = max(DEP_DELAY, na.rm=T)
    )
  return(desStat)
}

funBASE <- function(data){
  fourNumSum <- function(x){
    MIN_DELAY = min(x, na.rm=T)
    MEAN_DELAY = mean(x, na.rm=T)
    MEDIAN_DELAY = median(x, na.rm=T)
    MAX_DELAY = max(x, na.rm=T)
    return(c(MIN_DELAY=MIN_DELAY,MEAN_DELAY=MEAN_DELAY,
    MEDIAN_DELAY=MEDIAN_DELAY,MAX_DELAY=MAX_DELAY))
  }

  desStat <- with(data, aggregate(DEP_DELAY,
  list(ORIGIN,MONTH), fourNumSum))
  return(desStat)
}

library(microbenchmark)
microbenchmark(funDPLYR(data = USAairlineData2016),
funBASE(data = USAairlineData2016),
times = 1)
```

How it works…

In *step 2* from the previous section, it takes the entire dataset USAairlineData2016 as an input and passes it through the select() function to keep only the variables that are relevant to this recipe. After that, it creates groups by taking each unique combination of origin and month variable. It then calculates summary statistics such as minimum, mean, median, and maximum of departure delay. The first few rows of the output from *step 2* are given as follows:

```
> head(desStat)
Source: local data frame [6 x 6]
Groups: ORIGIN [1]

  ORIGIN MONTH MIN_DELAY MEAN_DELAY MEDIAN_DELAY MAX_DELAY
   <chr> <int>     <int>      <dbl>        <dbl>     <int>
1    ABE     1       -13   9.994186           -2       374
2    ABE     2       -15  15.841772           -3       449
3    ABE     4       -14   1.386905           -3       229
4    ABE     5       -15   2.777778           -4       150
5    ABE     6       -12   9.200837           -4       460
6    ABE     7       -16  22.064103           -1      1015
```

The default aggregate function in base R does not have the capacity to calculate more than one summary statistic at a time. However, it can take a customized function as an argument through FUN=. So, in *step 3*, you need a new customized function that will take a numeric vector as input and calculate the minimum, mean, median, and maximum of the input vector. You can then pass this newly defined function through aggregate to get the desired output. The new function fourNumSum in *step 3* is doing this calculation within aggregate. Here is the output of the calculation:

```
> head(desStat2)
  Group.1 Group.2 x.MIN_DELAY x.MEAN_DELAY x.MEDIAN_DELAY x.MAX_DELAY
1     ABE       1  -13.000000     9.994186      -2.000000  374.000000
2     ABQ       1  -24.000000     5.833799      -2.500000 1274.000000
3     ABR       1  -15.000000    11.354839       0.000000  507.000000
4     ABY       1  -12.000000     4.797468      -5.000000  182.000000
5     ACT       1  -21.000000    -1.710345      -8.000000  211.000000
6     ACV       1  -18.000000    14.025210       0.000000  121.000000
```

Now, in *step 4*, to compare the performances of the base R approach and the `dplyr` approach, you need to use the `microbenchmark` library and the function from that library to calculate the elapsed time by each approache. To do so, you need to define two new functions that will perform the summary statistics calculation in both approaches. In *step 4*, the `funDPLYR` function uses the functionality of the `dplyr` library and `funBASE` uses the base R functionality. Once you pass these two functions through `microbenchmark()`, you will be able to see the elapsed time taken by both approaches. Here is the output of the `microbenchmark()` function:

```
Unit: milliseconds
                              expr       min        lq      mean    median        uq       max neval
 funDPLYR(data = USAairlineData2016)  610.8936  617.5345  653.9049  620.4019  644.4227  820.4358    10
  funBASE(data = USAairlineData2016) 7887.7845 7972.5954 8125.8272 8055.7846 8226.4709 8801.3336    10
```

After repeating the same calculation 10 times, `neval` shows the time required to perform the task using both functions. From the output, it is quite obvious that the `dplyr` approach is taking less time compared to its base R counterpart.

There's more...

In this recipe, you went through the implementation using the `dplyr` approach and the base R approach. Though the outputs are same, if you notice the column name of the output, there is a difference between the approaches. This is one of the limitations of using the aggregate function. It usually treats all columns under the same name irrespective of the name you define in the customized function. As a result, the column name comes with an x prefix, whereas in the `dplyr` approach, the column name comes as you defined it within the body of the code.

Moreover, the output of the `dplyr` approach looks cleaner compared to the base R approach.

See also

To learn more about using `dplyr`, you can take a look at the documentation from the following sources:

- https://cran.r-project.org/web/packages/dplyr/index.html
- https://www.r-bloggers.com/using-r-quickly-calculating-summary-statistics-with-dplyr/

Using the customized function within the dplyr verbs

It is almost obvious that there is a need to write customized functions to solve specialized problems. Though there are lots of built-in functions available in base R and also in the specialized libraries, you still might require some kind of output that is not available through the built-in functions. For example, you might want to create a new output dataset by taking only the regression coefficient from a series of linear regression models for the various unique combinations of other variables. In that case, you must write a customized function to achieve this task. The `summarize()` function from the `dplyr` library is a convenient way to calculate user-defined statistics. The problem with the `summarize()` function within the `dplyr` library is that it can only return single-valued outputs.

In this recipe, you will write a customized function that will calculate the summary statistics (minimum, mean, median, and maximum) of a given variable for different combinations of other variables. The task is to pass the newly defined function through the `dplyr` functionality which will act like the `summarize()` function, but can produce multi-valued outputs.

Getting ready

To give you an idea of how to use a customized function within `dplyr` `summarize()` like functionality, the USA domestic airline dataset has been used. The objective is to calculate summary statistics (minimum, mean, median, and maximum) of the variables of interest over a possible combination of two other variables.

How to do it...

Here are the following few steps to complete this recipe:

1. Import the dataset.
2. Write the customized function.
3. Use the newly defined function in the `dplyr` framework.

Here are the necessary code blocks to implement all the preceding three steps:

```
USAairlineData2016 <- read.csv("USAairlineData2016.csv", as.is
= T)

# the new customized function to calculate summary statistics
fourNumSum <- function(x){
 MIN_DELAY = min(x, na.rm=T)
 MEAN_DELAY = mean(x, na.rm=T)
 MEDIAN_DELAY = median(x, na.rm=T)
 MAX_DELAY = max(x, na.rm=T)
 return(data.frame(MIN_DELAY=MIN_DELAY, MEAN_DELAY=MEAN_DELAY,
 MEDIAN_DELAY=MEDIAN_DELAY, MAX_DELAY=MAX_DELAY))
 }
```

4. Now, the `fourNumSum` function will be used within the `dplyr` framework to carry out the task as follows:

```
desStat <- USAairlineData2016 %>%
 select(MONTH, ORIGIN, DEP_DELAY) %>%
 group_by(ORIGIN, MONTH) %>%
 do(fourNumSum(.$DEP_DELAY))
```

5. The new object `desStat` will contain the output and the summary statistics of the `DEP_DELAY` variable using the `fourNumSum` function that has been applied over all possible combinations of the `ORIGIN` and `MONTH` variables.

How it works...

In the first place, the new function `fourNumSum` has been defined that produces multi-valued output as a data frame. Later, this function has been passed through the `dplyr` framework. The code works as follows:

At the start of the `dplyr` framework code, it takes the entire dataset `USAairlineData2016` as an input, and then, it passes through the `select()` function. Inside the `select()` function, it only keeps the variable of interest such as `MONTH`, `ORIGIN`, and `DEP_DELAY`. Then, it creates groups by taking all possible combinations of the `ORIGIN` and `MONTH` variables. After that, inside the `do()` function, it calls the user-defined customized function `fourNumSum`.

Note that, inside the do() function, a dot (.) and the dollar ($) sign are used. The dot is the placeholder for the input data frame, and the dollar sign is to specify the variable of interest for the fourNumSum function. The output of this function is given as follows:

```
> head(desStat)
Source: local data frame [6 x 6]
Groups: ORIGIN, MONTH [6]

  ORIGIN MONTH MIN_DELAY MEAN_DELAY MEDIAN_DELAY MAX_DELAY
   <chr> <int>     <int>      <dbl>        <dbl>     <int>
1    ABE     1       -13   9.994186           -2       374
2    ABE     2       -15  15.841772           -3       449
3    ABE     4       -14   1.386905           -3       229
4    ABE     5       -15   2.777778           -4       150
5    ABE     6       -12   9.200837           -4       460
6    ABE     7       -16  22.064103           -1      1015
```

There's more...

You might think that we could use the newly defined function within the dplyr framework just like the other function inside the summarize() function, but there is a problem in using the multi-valued function within summarize(). Here is an example of the use of the customized multi-valued function within the summarize() function:

```
desStat <- USAairlineData2016 %>%
select(MONTH, ORIGIN, DEP_DELAY) %>%
group_by(ORIGIN, MONTH) %>%
summarise(
fourNumSum(DEP_DELAY)
)
```

If you run the preceding code, you will get an error as shown in the following screenshot:

```
> desStat <- USAairlineData2016 %>%
+   select(MONTH, ORIGIN, DEP_DELAY) %>%
+   group_by(ORIGIN, MONTH) %>%
+   summarise(
+     fourNumSum(DEP_DELAY)
+   )
Error in eval(substitute(expr), envir, enclos) : expecting a single value
>
```

The `summarise()` verb is expecting a function that can produce a single-valued output, but the function that has been used is producing a multi-valued output, and as a result, the error is being generated by the R process.

See also

If you want to perform any arbitrary operation in the `dplyr` framework, then you must use the `do()` function from the `dplyr` library. To get more details on using `do()`, you can take a look at the documentation by typing `?do` in the R console.

Using the select verb for data processing

The dataset usually contains a large number of variables that are not relevant for every type of analysis. Working with the entire dataset consumes more memory, and it is recommended that you use only the smaller number of variables for the analysis that is required to achieve the task. Taking the smaller number of variables from the entire dataset is usually known as **subsetting**, but when the term subset has been used, the user could interpret this in two ways: subset of dataset with a smaller number of variables and also subset by taking fewer rows from the entire dataset. In the `dplyr` library, these two aspects are covered by the `select()` and `filter()` verbs. In this recipe, you will subset a dataset by taking only a handful of variables by using the `select()` verb.

Getting ready

Whenever it comes to the issue of working with a smaller number of variables from the original bigger dataset, it is better to do the task on the fly. You can create another data frame by taking a small number of variables, but again it will consume extra memory. Rather than creating a new data frame by taking a few variables, you can perform the operation on the fly using the `select()` verb of `dplyr`. In this recipe, you will apply the `select()` verb to create a subset of the original `USAairlineData2016` dataset by taking only the following variables:

- `QUARTER`
- `MONTH`
- `ORIGIN`

- DEST
- DEP_DELAY
- ARR_DELAY

How to do it...

Let's take a look at the following steps to see how we can use the select() verb for data processing:

1. The first step is always to import the dataset and then do the specific operation. Here is the code to import the dataset and then use the select() verb to subset the dataset on the fly. There are other operators also shown in this task. For example, fitting a linear regression model of arrival delay with departure delay for each quarter as follows:

```
USAairlineData2016 <- read.csv("USAairlineData2016.csv", as.is
= T)

selectExample <- USAairlineData2016 %>%
select(QUARTER, MONTH, ORIGIN, DEST, DEP_DELAY, ARR_DELAY) %>%
group_by(QUARTER) %>%
do(regModel = lm(ARR_DELAY ~ DEP_DELAY, data=.)) %>%
summarise(intercept = coef(regModel)[1], regCoef =
coef(regModel)[2])
```

2. To select the subset of variables using the base R functionality, the corresponding code is as follows:

```
selectExample2 <- USAairlineData2016[c("QUARTER", "MONTH",
"ORIGIN", "DEST", "DEP_DELAY", "ARR_DELAY")]
```

How it works...

In the dplyr framework, the first input is the entire dataset which works like the attach() function in base R. The use of the pipe operator gives you the facility to call the variable names without any quote similar to accessing the variables after applying the attach() function. The select() function takes the first input as the entire data frame and then takes the names of variables separated by commas. In this example, the variables were QUARTER, MONTH, ORIGIN, DEST, DEP_DELAY, and ARR_DELAY.

To show the significance of using `select()`, the example has more code such as `group_by()`, `do()`, and `summarize()`. These additional three functions have been used to show the capability of processing larger datasets efficiently and on the fly. There is no need to create an intermediate data frame for performing further analysis.

In the preceding example from the previous section, a linear regression model has been fitted between arrival delay and departure delay for each quarter of the year 2016, and the resultant intercept and slope have been collected into a data frame. If you want to do the same operation using the base R functionality, you need more memory and processing time compared to the `dplyr` framework.

There's more...

The `select()` function has more facilities. For example, you can select multiple adjacent variables by writing only the first and last variable name in the sequence, separated by a colon as follows:

```
select(YEAR:DAY_OF_WEEK)
```

The preceding code will select all variables in between YEAR and DAY_OF_WEEK, including these two variables. If you want to exclude some variables, then this task can be done using a negative sign before writing a variable name as follows:

```
select(-YEAR)
```

It will select all variables in the dataset, except the variable YEAR.

If you need to rename certain variables during the subset, you can easily do that within the `select()` function. The general structure to rename a variable during selection is as follows:

```
select(new_name = old_name)
```

See also

It could happen that you do not know the exact name of the variables, but you know the partial name. You can still select the variables just using the partial variable names, but you need to use the following functions within the `select()` operation:

- `starts_with()`
- `ends_with()`
- `matches()`
- `contains()`

You will get more information about those wild card functions by typing `?starts_with` in the R console.

Using the filter verb for data processing

The subset of a dataset can be created in the following two ways with two different perspectives:

- Subset of rows only
- Subset of columns only

To select subset of rows only, the `filter()` verb has been used, and this is faster than its base R counterpart. In this recipe, you will subset a data frame by selecting rows based on certain conditions. Again, this operation can be done on the fly without the need to create a new data frame.

Getting ready

The objective is to create a subset of data frame by taking only those flights that have more than 30 minutes delay. In other words, the subset will contain all the variables from the original dataset, but fewer rows that satisfy the condition that departure delay is more than 30 minutes. We have used `USAairlineData2016` for this recipe.

How to do it...

Let's take a look at the following steps to see how we can use the `filter()` verb for data processing:

1. Import the dataset from the CSV file and then apply the `filter()` verb from the `dplyr` library as follows:

   ```
   USAairlineData2016 <- read.csv("USAairlineData2016.csv", as.is
   = T)

   filterExample <- USAairlineData2016 %>%
   filter(DEP_DELAY>30)
   ```

2. Alternatively, the `filter()` code can be written without using the pipe operator as follows:

   ```
   filterExample2 <- filter(USAairlineData2016, DEP_DELAY>30)
   ```

3. The base R functionality to achieve a similar task is as follows:

   ```
   filterExample3 <- USAairlineData2016
   [USAairlineData2016$DEP_DELAY>30,]
   ```

   However, the base R approach takes a bit longer than the `dplyr` approach.

How it works...

Like other verbs in `dplyr`, `filter()` takes the first input as the data frame and then executes the conditional statement. The output dataset contains only those rows that satisfy the condition provided within the `filter()` function. The conditional part could take any valid complex condition that produces only a TRUE/FALSE response.

Using the arrange verb for data processing

In the data pre-processing steps, sorting the rows based on a variable of interest is one of the most common tasks. The `dplyr` verb `arrange()` works in a very similar way to the base R `sort()` function, but it has more intuitive features than default `sort()`. In this recipe, you will use the verb `arrange()` to organize the rows of a data frame.

Getting ready

The original USAairlineData2016 function has been sorted based on QUARTER and MONTH, but in this recipe, the task is to organize the rows based on the origin of the flight, and then, the second level sorting will be done on destination. Once again, the same dataset will be used in this recipe.

How to do it...

The steps to use the arrange() verb are very simple and intuitive. The following are the steps:

1. Import the dataset into the R environment.
2. Call the arrange() function.
3. Provide the entire data frame as input.
4. Specify the variable names.

    Here is the actual code to implement the steps:

    ```
    arrangeExample <- arrange(USAairlineData2016, ORIGIN, DEST)
    ```

5. If you are interested to do sorting in descending order, then you must use the desc() function within the arrange() verb as follows:

    ```
    arrangeExample2 <- arrange(USAairlineData2016, ORIGIN,
    desc(DEST))
    ```

6. The base R alternative code to sort the rows is as follows:

    ```
    sortRows <- USAairlineData2016[order(USAairlineData2016$ORIGIN,
    USAairlineData2016$DEST),]
    ```

How it works...

The `arrange()` verb takes the first input argument as a data frame and then, the names of variables to organize the rows in ascending order. In the code, it takes `USAairlineData2016` as input data and the `ORIGIN` and `DEST` variables for organizing the rows in ascending order. To do the descending arrangement, the `desc()` function has been used. The `arrange()` verb works relatively slower than other verbs in `dplyr`, but it works faster than the base R `order()` function.

There's more...

If you wish to use the variable name as a vector of string, then you must use the `arrange()` verb with an underscore (_) as a suffix as follows:

```
arrangeExample3 <- arrange_(USAairlineData2016, .dots=c("ORIGIN",
"DEST"))
```

Using mutate for data processing

Creating a new variable is one of the most important tasks in data pre-processing. Creating a new variable and getting it attached to the new variable with existing data frame is called **mutation** in the `dplyr` framework. The verb `mutate()` is used to achieve this task. In this recipe, you will create a new variable from an existing data frame using the `mutate()` verb. Also, you will see the base R counter example using the `transform()` function.

Getting ready

The task of this recipe is to create a new indicator variable that indicates whether the flight has more than 30 minutes delay, or not. The `USAairlineData2016` dataset will be used for this recipe. The newly created variable should be attached with the existing data frame.

How to do it...

Like all other `dplyr` verbs, mutate also takes the first input as a data frame. Here are the steps to create a new variable using the `mutate()` verb:

1. Import the dataset into the R environment.
2. Create a new variable within the `mutate()` verb and give a new name to the variable that has been created.
3. Assign the resultant data frame to a new name.

   Here is the implementation:

   ```
   USAairlineData2016 <- read.csv("USAairlineData2016.csv", as.is
   = T)
   USAairlineData2016 <- mutate(USAairlineData2016, delayIndicator
   = DEP_DELAY>30)
   ```

4. The alternative base R implementation for the same task is as follows:

   ```
   USAairlineData2016$delayIndicator <-
   USAairlineData2016$DEP_DELAY>30
   ```

5. You can also write it as follows:

   ```
   USAairlineData2016$delayIndicator <-
   ifelse(USAairlineData2016$DEP_DELAY>30,1,0)
   ```

How it works...

The `mutate()` verb takes the data frame as an input, and then, it performs the operation defined within the verb. In this example, the operation was to create a new logical variable indicating whether the flight has more than 30 minutes delay in departure. Within the `mutate()` verb, you can define any valid new variable, and this operation can be combined with other `dplyr` verbs such as `group_by()`, `filter()`, `select()`, and so on.

The base R implementation looks pretty simple, but it takes longer than the `dplyr` counterpart. There is another base R alternative to create the new variable `transform()`. The advantage of `mutate()` over `transform()` is that you can use the newly created variable within the same `mutate()` verb, but it is not possible to use `transform()`. Here is an example of this facility:

```
USAairlineData2016 <- mutate(USAairlineData2016,
diffDepArr = (ARR_DELAY - DEP_DELAY),
diffDepArrCat = diffDepArr>0)
```

In the preceding code, first, the new variable `diffDepArr` has been created by taking the difference between the arrival delay and departure delay. Also, within the same `mutate()` verb, the newly created variable has been used to create another new variable. This type of operation is not possible using the `transform()` function.

There's more...

Similar to the `mutate()` verb, there is another verb such as `transmute()`. The `mutate()` verb creates a new variable while retaining the existing variables within the data frame, whereas `transmute()` drops the existing variable and only keeps newly created variables.

Using summarise to summarize dataset

It might sound as though the `summarise()` verb can only produce summary (descriptive) statistics, but it has a more generic application. You can use the `summarise()` verb to perform the following types of operation:

- You can perform a single operation on a single variable
- You can perform a single operation on multiple variables
- You can perform multiple operations on a single variable
- You can also perform multiple operations on multiple variables

In this recipe, you will see examples for each type of application of the `summarise()` verb.

Getting ready

Let's consider that you are interested in calculating descriptive statistics of departure delay and arrival delay of the `USAairlineData2016` dataset for each group of the `ORIGIN` and `DESTINATION` variables. The variables of interest in this recipe are as follows:

- `ORIGIN`
- `DEST`
- `DEP_DELAY`
- `ARR_DELAY`

You will implement all the scenarios listed in the introduction of this recipe.

How to do it...

Let's take a look at the following steps and learn how to use the `summarise()` verb to summarize the dataset:

1. In the first step, import the dataset into the R environment as follows:

```
USAairlineData2016 <- read.csv("USAairlineData2016.csv", as.is
= T)
```

2. Now, we will take a look at the following four scenarios that depict all the operations mentioned in the beginning of this recipe:

- **One operation on one variable**: The `summarise()` verb will take the input of a single variable and produce a single-valued output. In the following example, it takes the `DEP_DELAY` variable as an input and produces mean delay as an output:

```
meanDelay <- USAairlineData2016 %>%
 select(ORIGIN, DEST, DEP_DELAY) %>%
 group_by(ORIGIN,DEST) %>%
 summarise(meanDelay = mean(DEP_DELAY, na.rm=T))
```

The preceding code snippet generates the following output:

```
> meanDelay
Source: local data frame [4,582 x 3]
Groups: ORIGIN [?]

   ORIGIN  DEST meanDelay
```

```
        <chr> <chr>    <dbl>
1       ABE   ATL  11.631414
2       ABE   DTW  11.010989
3       ABE   EWR  69.000000
4       ABE   ORD   9.882812
5       ABI   DFW   9.968354
6       ABQ   ATL   4.350978
7       ABQ   AUS   3.344828
8       ABQ   BWI   8.141856
9       ABQ   DAL   8.126919
10      ABQ   DEN   5.356260
# ... with 4,572 more rows
```

- **One operation on multiple variables**: The `summarise()` verb will take more than one variable as an input, and then, it will produce the same type of statistic as the output. In the following example, it takes two variables as input and produces a single statistic (mean) for both of the variables:

```
meanDelay2 <- USAairlineData2016 %>%
  select(ORIGIN, DEST, DEP_DELAY, ARR_DELAY) %>%
  group_by(ORIGIN,DEST) %>%
  summarise(meanDelay = mean(DEP_DELAY, na.rm=T),
  meanArrival = mean(ARR_DELAY, na.rm=T))
```

The preceding code snippet generates the following output:

```
> meanDelay2
Source: local data frame [4,582 x 4]
Groups: ORIGIN [?]

    ORIGIN  DEST meanDelay meanArrival
    <chr> <chr>     <dbl>       <dbl>
1     ABE   ATL  11.631414   0.8277311
2     ABE   DTW  11.010989   6.5193370
3     ABE   EWR  69.000000  56.0000000
4     ABE   ORD   9.882812   7.6703297
5     ABI   DFW   9.968354  10.2547771
6     ABQ   ATL   4.350978  -5.7220300
7     ABQ   AUS   3.344828   3.0344828
8     ABQ   BWI   8.141856  -0.3661972
9     ABQ   DAL   8.126919   5.2205098
10    ABQ   DEN   5.356260  -0.1260141
# ... with 4,572 more rows
```

- **Multiple operations on a single variable**: The `summarise()` verb takes a single variable as an input and calculates multiple values as output. In the following example, it takes only one variable as input, but it produces mean and standard deviation as the output:

```
summaryStat <- USAairlineData2016 %>%
select(ORIGIN, DEST, DEP_DELAY, ARR_DELAY) %>%
group_by(ORIGIN,DEST) %>%
summarise(meanDelay = mean(DEP_DELAY, na.rm=T),
sdDelay = sd(DEP_DELAY, na.rm=T))
```

The preceding code snippet generates the following output:

```
> summaryStat
Source: local data frame [4,582 x 4]
Groups: ORIGIN [?]

   ORIGIN  DEST meanDelay   sdDelay
    <chr> <chr>     <dbl>     <dbl>
1     ABE   ATL 11.631414  63.87788
2     ABE   DTW 11.010989  55.04421
3     ABE   EWR 69.000000       NaN
4     ABE   ORD  9.882812  42.13775
5     ABI   DFW  9.968354  42.78377
6     ABQ   ATL  4.350978  32.88694
7     ABQ   AUS  3.344828  14.01345
8     ABQ   BWI  8.141856  30.84078
9     ABQ   DAL  8.126919  28.83888
10    ABQ   DEN  5.356260  31.09194
# ... with 4,572 more rows
```

- **Multiple operations on multiple variables**: The `summarise()` verb takes multiple variables as input and also produces multi-valued outputs:

```
summaryStat2 <- USAairlineData2016 %>%
 select(ORIGIN, DEST, DEP_DELAY, ARR_DELAY) %>%
 group_by(ORIGIN,DEST) %>%
 summarise(meanDelay = mean(DEP_DELAY, na.rm=T),
 sdDelay = sd(DEP_DELAY, na.rm=T),
 meanArrival = mean(ARR_DELAY, na.rm=T),
 sdArrival = sd(ARR_DELAY, na.rm=T))
```

The preceding code snippet generates the following output:

```
> summaryStat2
Source: local data frame [4,582 x 6]
Groups: ORIGIN [?]

   ORIGIN  DEST meanDelay  sdDelay meanArrival sdArrival
    <chr> <chr>     <dbl>    <dbl>       <dbl>     <dbl>
1     ABE   ATL 11.631414 63.87788   0.8277311  65.09406
2     ABE   DTW 11.010989 55.04421   6.5193370  54.27295
3     ABE   EWR 69.000000      NaN  56.0000000       NaN
4     ABE   ORD  9.882812 42.13775   7.6703297  45.76634
5     ABI   DFW  9.968354 42.78377  10.2547771  45.84001
6     ABQ   ATL  4.350978 32.88694  -5.7220300  34.16882
7     ABQ   AUS  3.344828 14.01345   3.0344828  14.97017
8     ABQ   BWI  8.141856 30.84078  -0.3661972  31.88637
9     ABQ   DAL  8.126919 28.83888   5.2205098  29.95560
10    ABQ   DEN  5.356260 31.09194  -0.1260141  31.78422
# ... with 4,572 more rows
```

How it works...

For each of the scenarios, it takes the data frame as input and then performs the operations. The examples that we saw in the previous section give us a clear indication of the flexibility of the summarise() verb and its powerful use in the context of big data. To achieve the same objective as you have done in the example from the previous section using the base R functionality, you will require more memory and processing power. However, the summarise() verb in the dplyr library easily handles larger datasets.

7
R for Text Processing

Every day, we are producing a huge amount of text data, either structured or unstructured plain format through various media such as Facebook, Twitter, Blog posts, or even scientific research articles. In the financial market, the sentiment of people plays a vital role. You can mine sentiment by analyzing text data obtained from various sources. In this chapter, you will learn the recipe related to working with unstructured text data. This chapter will cover the following recipes:

- Extracting unstructured text data from a plain web page
- Extracting text data from an HTML page
- Extracting text data from an HTML page using the XML library
- Extracting text data from PubMed
- Importing unstructured text data from a plain text file
- Importing plain text data from a PDF file
- Pre-processing text data for topic modeling and sentiment analysis
- Creating a word cloud to explore unstructured text data
- Using regular expression in text processing

Introduction

In the current internet era, the amount of data is increasing at a rapid speed. There are various forms of data we produce every day. Text data is one of the most important sources of data for uncovering knowledge. In the medical field, biomedical text mining is one of the most important applications of text data for studying diseases, genes, protein relations, and drug discovery. In the financial market, the microblog, such as Twitter, plays an important role in uncovering people's sentiment about the market. Also, every day, a large number of scientific research articles are being published in various journals, and this is also a great source of text data. By doing text mining on scientific research articles, one can easily identify current research trends, important keywords, and links between entities.

Before actually performing the text mining, you should learn how to retrieve text data from various sources. This chapter is dedicated to walking you through text data retrieval from various sources and some pre-processing.

Extracting unstructured text data from a plain web page

In the age of the internet revolution, web pages are the most popular source of text data. You can get newspaper articles, blog posts, personal biography web pages, and many more. Articles in Wikipedia are another source of plain text data through Wikipedia web pages. In this recipe, you will learn how to extract text data from a plain web page.

Getting ready

In this recipe, to extract unstructured text data from a plain web page, the following web page will be used:

```
https://en.wikipedia.org/wiki/Programming_with_Big_Data_in_R
```

This page contains a brief description of programming with big data in R. The objective is to read the web page using R and store the text data into an R object. Here is a partial screenshot of the page:

How to do it...

To read an unstructured text data from a web page using the most naïve R approach, perform the following steps:

1. Create a character object containing the web page address in the form of an URL.
2. Create a connection with the link using the `url()` function from the base library.
3. Read the source code of the web page line by line. Then, the resultant object will contain all the source code of the web page in the form of a character vector. The length of the vector will be equal to the number of lines into the source code of the HTML web page:

```
# Creating an object containing the link to the webpage
sourceURL <-
"https://en.wikipedia.org/wiki/Programming_with_Big_Data_in_R"

# Creating an active connection between R session and webpage
# Internet connection required
link2web <- url(sourceURL)
```

```
# Reading line by line html source code
htmlText <- readLines(link2web)

# close the connection between R session and webpage
close(link2web)
```

How it works...

This is the simplest approach to reading text data from a web page. The steps are very simple and intuitive to understand. The url() function creates a connection link between the web page and R session, and then it reads the text line by line through the readLines() function. Since the code reads the HTML source code line by line, the resultant object is a vector of character. Each line contains the HTML source code from the original HTML web page.

Though the output object contains HTML code, you are not able to do further processing assuming an HTML structure. The output object is a completely unstructured text vector. Here is the output of the first few lines:

```
> head(htmlText)
[1] "<!DOCTYPE html>"
[2] "<html class=\"client-nojs\" lang=\"en\" dir=\"ltr\">"
[3] "<head>"
[4] "<meta charset=\"UTF-8\"/>"
[5] "<title>Programming with Big Data in R - Wikipedia</title>"
[6] "<script>document.documentElement.className = document.documentElement.className.replace( /(^|\\s)client-nojs(\\s|$)/, \"$1client-js$2\" );</script>"
> |
```

From the preceding output, it is clear that to do any further analysis, there is a need to do pre-processing, which is a time-consuming task.

There's more...

The readLines() function can read the source code of a web page as you have seen in this example. This function also reads data from a file stored into the local computer. To read the data from the local file, you have to create the connection using the file() function instead of url(). The url() function is specific to creating a connection with a web page, but file() is for creating a connection with a local file.

Extracting text data from an HTML page

You have seen an example of reading the HTML source code as a text vector in the *Extracting unstructured text data from a plain web page* recipe in this chapter. In this recipe, further processing is not straightforward because the output object contains plain text as well as HTML code tags. It is a time-consuming task to clean up the HTML tags from plain text.

In this recipe, you will read the same web page from the following link:

```
https://en.wikipedia.org/wiki/Programming_with_Big_Data_in_R
```

However, this time, you will use a different strategy so that you can play with HTML tags.

Getting ready

To implement this recipe, you need to use a customized library, particularly, the rvest library. If this library has not been installed into your computer, then this is the time to install it with its necessary dependencies. Here is the code to install the rvest library:

```
install.packages("rvest", dependencies = T)
```

Once the installation has been completed, you are ready to implement this recipe.

How to do it...

The steps to implement this recipe are as follows:

1. Load the rvest library. This is a specialized library for reading and processing HTML web pages.
2. Create an object containing the URL as a character string.
3. Call the read_html() function and pass the object containing the URL.

   The code for the preceding steps is as follows:

   ```
   library(rvest)
   sourceURL <-
   "https://en.wikipedia.org/wiki/Programming_with_Big_Data_in_R"
   htmlTextData <- read_html(sourceURL)
   ```

How it works...

Unlike `readLines()`, the `read_html()` function does not read the source code line by line, rather it reads the entire HTML source code into a single object while maintaining the original HTML structure. If you want to see the output of the HTML source code, you have to retrieve the plain text component under various HTML tags.

The `rvest` library has functions to interact with various HTML tags and retrieve the plain text elements from it. For example, suppose you are interested in retrieving the title of the web page. The title of the page has been enclosed by the `<title>...</title>` HTML tag pair. The following code will give you the plain text title of the page:

```
html_text(html_nodes(htmlTextData,xpath="//title"))
```

Notice that there are two functions that have been used in this line, `html_nodes()` and then `html_text()`. The first function `html_nodes()` is for extracting the nodes that have the `<title>...</title>` tag pair. Once the internal HTML nodes have been extracted, then it parses through the `html_text()` function to retrieve the plain text component of the nodes. In this case, you will get the title of the page as follows:

```
> html_text(html_nodes(htmlTextData,xpath="//title"))
[1] "Programming with Big Data in R - Wikipedia"
```

Now, once you have the page title extracted as plain text, you can easily store it in an object. The next thing you might want is to extract the paragraph text. There are several paragraphs on this web page and you can capture all of them using the `<p>...</p>` tag pair as follows:

```
html_text(html_nodes(htmlTextData,xpath="//p"))
```

There's more...

To read text data from HTML pages, you could also use the XML library. The code structure is somewhat similar, but `rvest` is more popular and powerful.

To interact all nodes based on a single tag pair, the `html_nodes()` function will be useful, but if you are interested only in one node (the very first node) of a tag pair, then you can use the `html_node()` function and then pass the output through `html_text()` to get plain text output.

Extracting text data from an HTML page using the XML library

The XML library is another R library for extracting text data from the HTML web page. In the previous recipes, you saw how to extract text from a web page using `readLines()` and then using the `rvest` library. In this recipe, you will go through the functions of the XML library to extract the same data.

Getting ready

Before using the XML library, you have to install it into your computer. To install the XML library, you can use the following code:

```
install.packages("XML", dependencies = T)
```

Once the installation is completed, you are ready to implement this recipe.

How to do it...

The HTML file is a tree-like structure. It represents the data using various internal nodes. Each node is represented by tag pair, such as `<p>...</p>`. The steps are as follows:

1. Create an R object containing the character string of the website address.
2. Load the XML library into your R session.
3. Parse the link into the `htmlTreeParse()` function, and make sure you have mentioned `useInternalNodes=TRUE`.
4. To get an exact plain text value from the HTML tree, you can use the `xpathSApply()` function with HTML tag pairs.

The R code corresponding to the preceding steps is as follows:

```
library(XML)
sourceURL <-
"https://en.wikipedia.org/wiki/Programming_with_Big_Data_in_R"
link2web <- url(sourceURL)
htmlText <- readLines(link2web)
close(link2web)
html_doc <- htmlTreeParse(htmlText,useInternalNodes=T)
pageTitle <- xpathSApply(html_doc,"//title",xmlValue)
```

How it works...

The XML library has a function called `htmlTreeParse()`. This function is able to read the HTML tree structure directly. However, in some cases, you might not get the expected results, and the function produces a warning report into the R console as follows:

```
htmldocTree <- htmlTreeParse(sourceURL, useInternalNodes = T)
Warning message:
  XML content does not seem to be XML:
    'https://en.wikipedia.org/wiki/Programming_with_Big_Data_in_R'
```

To overcome this limitation, you can use one simple trick. First, read the HTML source code as a vector of text and then create an HTML tree structure using the `htmlTreeParse()` function. In this recipe, we have followed this method. First, `readLines()` creates a vector of text with HTML source code, and then it parses through the `htmlTreeParse()` function to create an HTML tree structure. Once you have created a tree structure, you are able to extract plain text using HTML tag pairs. To retrieve plain text under the tag pair `<title>` ... `</title>`, the following code has been used:

```
html_doc <- htmlTreeParse(htmlText,useInternalNodes=T)
pageTitle <- xpathSApply(html_doc,"//title",xmlValue)
```

Extracting text data from PubMed

PubMed is one of the most important sources of text data containing scientific research papers. If you want to see the current trend of research in a topic, you can do so by doing a literature review. Using R, you will be able to search scientific papers through PubMed and then extract the title of the paper, journal name, and even the abstract text for further analysis. In this recipe, you will perform a literature search and retrieve abstracts along with the title and journal name and year of publication.

Getting ready

You will require the following two libraries to run this recipe:

- `pubmed.mineR`
- `RISmed`

To install the preceding two libraries along with their dependencies, execute the following code:

```
install.packages(c("pubmed.mineR", "RISmed"), dependencies = TRUE)
```

The next thing for this recipe is to decide on the `keyword` term for the PubMed search. Let's say you are interested in performing a literature search that uses `"Deep Learning"` as `keyword`.

How to do it...

Let's perform the following steps to perform a PubMed literature search using R:

1. Load the `pubmed.mineR` and `RISmed` libraries into your R session.
2. Create an object containing keywords.
3. Parse the `keyword` term to create a query term into the form of PubMed `search_query`.
4. Parse the `search_query` term to get the search results.
5. Retrieve the relevant information from the output objects.

    Here is the code to perform the preceding tasks mentioned:

    ```
    library(pubmed.mineR)
    library(RISmed)
    keyword <- "Deep Learning"
    search_query <- EUtilsSummary(keyword, retmax=10)
    summary(search_query)
    fetch <- EUtilsGet(search_query)
    ```

6. The `fetch` object contains all the information you might be interested in. Here is the list of objects that you can extract from it:

```
> getSlots("Medline")
                Query                  PMID           YearReceived          MonthReceived            DayReceived
            "character"           "character"              "numeric"              "numeric"              "numeric"
         HourReceived        MinuteReceived           YearAccepted          MonthAccepted            DayAccepted
            "numeric"             "numeric"              "numeric"              "numeric"              "numeric"
         HourAccepted        MinuteAccepted           YearEpublish           MonthEpublish            DayEpublish
            "numeric"             "numeric"              "numeric"              "numeric"              "numeric"
         HourEpublish        MinuteEpublish           YearPpublish           MonthPpublish            DayPpublish
            "numeric"             "numeric"              "numeric"              "numeric"              "numeric"
         HourPpublish        MinutePpublish                YearPmc               MonthPmc                DayPmc
            "numeric"             "numeric"              "numeric"              "numeric"              "numeric"
              HourPmc             MinutePmc             YearPubmed            MonthPubmed             DayPubmed
            "numeric"             "numeric"              "numeric"              "numeric"              "numeric"
          HourPubmed          MinutePubmed                 Author                   ISSN                  Title
            "numeric"             "numeric"                 "list"            "character"            "character"
         ArticleTitle           ELocationID           AbstractText            Affiliation               Language
            "character"           "character"            "character"            "character"            "character"
      PublicationType             MedlineTA            NlmUniqueID            ISSNLinking      PublicationStatus
                "list"           "character"            "character"            "character"            "character"
            ArticleId                Volume                  Issue         ISOAbbreviation            MedlinePgn
            "character"           "character"            "character"            "character"            "character"
  CopyrightInformation               Country                GrantID                Acronym                 Agency
            "character"           "character"            "character"            "character"            "character"
       RegistryNumber             RefSource         CollectiveName                   Mesh
            "character"           "character"            "character"                 "list"
>
```

7. The `fetch` object that you have created contains a lot of internal information but you might be only interested in some of it. So, the next step is to retrieve some of the fields that you might be interested in, especially `Title`, `ArticleTitle`, `AbstractText,` and `YearPubmed` along with `PMID`:

```
pmid <- PMID(fetch)
years <- YearPubmed(fetch)
Jtitle <- Title(fetch)
articleTitle <- ArticleTitle(fetch)
abstracts <- AbstractText(fetch)
```

How it works...

Once you supply the keywords to the `EUtilsSummary()` function, it converts `keyword` into the PubMed `search_query` term. Inside the `EUtilsSummary()` function, you could mention the number of articles you want to retrieve. In this example, the number of articles is limited to `10` to save time. The output of the `EUtilsSummary()` function will look as follows:

```
> search_query
[1] "(\"DEEP Dev Educ Exch Pap\"[Journal] OR \"deep\"[All Fields])
AND (\"learning\"[MeSH Terms] OR \"learning\"[All Fields])"
```

The `keyword` term that has been used,`"Deep Learning"`, is now converted into PubMed `search_query`. The summary of the `search_query` term will tell you the number of articles available with the keywords that have been used. In this case, the number is `3849` as follows:

```
> summary(search_query)
Query:
   ("DEEP Dev Educ Exch Pap"[Journal] OR "deep"[All Fields]) AND
   ("learning"[MeSH Terms] OR "learning"[All Fields])

Result count:  3849
```

Upto now, the results are stored internally as R objects. The next step is to retrieve the following fields from the searched items:

- PubMed ID (`PMID`)
- Year of publication (`YearPubmed`)
- Journal title (`Title`)
- Article title (`ArticleTitle`)
- Abstract text (`AbstractText`)

All of the preceding fields have been extracted using the following block of code:

```
pmid <- PMID(fetch)
years <- YearPubmed(fetch)
Jtitle <- Title(fetch)
articleTitle <- ArticleTitle(fetch)
abstracts <- AbstractText(fetch)
```

Here is the truncated screenshot of the output:

```
> pmid
 [1] "28749969" "28748430" "28747353" "28744460" "28743752" "28742602" "28742048" "28742027" "28739578" "28736569"
> years
 [1] 2017 2017 2017 2017 2017 2017 2017 2017 2017 2017
> Jtitle
 [1] "PLoS computational biology"
 [2] "Journal of medical systems"
 [3] "CBE life sciences education"
 [4] "BioMed research international"
 [5] "Proceedings of the National Academy of Sciences of the United States of America"
 [6] "Clinical journal of sport medicine : official journal of the Canadian Academy of Sport Medicine"
 [7] "IEEE transactions on neural networks and learning systems"
 [8] "IEEE transactions on bio-medical engineering"
 [9] "Evidence-based mental health"
[10] "Frontiers in plant science"
> articleTitle
 [1] "TopologyNet: Topology based deep convolutional and multi-task neural networks for biomolecular property predictions."
 [2] "iNICU - Integrated Neonatal Care Unit: Capturing Neonatal Journey in an Intelligent Data Way."
 [3] "Effectiveness of a Low-Cost, Graduate Student-Led Intervention on Study Habits and Performance in Introductory Biology."
 [4] "Protein Function Prediction Using Deep Restricted Boltzmann Machines."
 [5] "Thalamocortical synchronization during induction and emergence from propofol-induced unconsciousness."
 [6] "Is There a Relationship Between the Functional Movement Screen, Star Excursion Balance Test, and Balance Error Scoring System?"
 [7] "Broad Learning System: An Effective and Efficient Incremental Learning System Without the Need for Deep Architecture."
 [8] "A regularized deep learning approach for clinical risk prediction of acute coronary syndrome using electronic health records."
 [9] "Applying deep neural networks to unstructured text notes in electronic medical records for phenotyping youth depression."
[10] "Deep Plant Phenomics: A Deep Learning Platform for Complex Plant Phenotyping Tasks."
> abstracts
 [1] "Although deep learning approaches have had tremendous success in image, video and audio processing, computer vision, and speech recognit
ion, their applications to three-dimensional (3D) biomolecular structural data sets have been hindered by the geometric and biological complex
ity. To address this problem we introduce the element-specific persistent homology (ESPH) method. ESPH represents 3D complex geometry by one-d
imensional (1D) topological invariants and retains important biological information via a multichannel image-like representation. This represe
ntation reveals hidden structure-function relationships in biomolecules. We further integrate ESPH and deep convolutional neural networks to c
onstruct a multichannel topological neural network (TopologyNet) for the predictions of protein-ligand binding affinities and protein stabilit
y changes upon mutation. To overcome the deep learning limitations from small and noisy training sets, we propose a multi-task multichannel to
pologi... <truncated>
```

There's more...

In this example, only a small number of fields have been extracted. You can extract more information such as author name, country of publication, publication type, and so on. The general structure of the code to extract the fields is as follows:

- `NameOfMethod` (the object that contains the retrieved search results)

For example, if you want to retrieve the list of author names, take a look at the following code:

```
> Author(fetch)
[[1]]
  LastName ForeName Initials order
1     Cang   Zixuan        Z     1
2      Wei   Guowei        G     2

[[2]]
    LastName ForeName Initials order
1      Singh Harpreet        H     1
2      Yadav   Gautam        G     2
3   Mallaiah Raghuram        R     3
4      Joshi  Preetha        P     4
```

```
5        Joshi      Vinay          V        5
6         Kaur    Ravneet          R        6
7       Bansal    Suneyna          S        7
8 Brahmachari    Samir K          SK        8

[[3]]
    LastName ForeName Initials order
1    Hoskins  Tyler D       TD     1
2      Gantz      J D       JD     2
3    Chaffee  Blake R       BR     3
4 Arlinghaus      Kel        K     4
5    Wiebler    James        J     5
6     Hughes  Michael        M     6
7  Fernandes  Joyce J       JJ     7

[[4]]
  LastName ForeName Initials order
1      Zou Xianchun        X     1
2     Wang   Guijun        G     2
3       Yu  Guoxian        G     3

[[5]]
   LastName      ForeName Initials order
1    Flores Francisco J        FJ     1
2 Hartnack Katharine E        KE     2
3     Fath    Amanda B        AB     3
4      Kim   Seong-Eun        SE     4
5   Wilson   Matthew A        MA     5
6    Brown    Emery N        EN     6
7   Purdon   Patrick L        PL     7

[[6]]
      LastName   ForeName Initials order
1 Harshbarger   Nicole D       ND     1
2    Anderson   Barton E       BE     2
3         Lam Kenneth C       KC     3

[[7]]
   LastName    ForeName Initials order
1     Chen C L Philip      CLP     1
2      Liu     Zhulin        Z     2

[[8]]
   LastName  ForeName Initials order
1     Huang Zhengxing        Z     1
2      Dong       Wei        W     2
3      Duan   Huilong        H     3
4       Liu    Jiquan        J     4
```

```
[[9]]
    LastName ForeName Initials order
1    Geraci   Joseph        J     1
2 Wilansky   Pamela         P     2
3  de Luca Vincenzo         V     3
4      Roy   Anvesh         A     4
5  Kennedy  James L        JL     5
6  Strauss     John         J     6

[[10]]
    LastName ForeName Initials order
1   Ubbens Jordan R       JR     1
2 Stavness      Ian        I     2
```

Importing unstructured text data from a plain text file

In some cases, it could happen that your source text data has been stored in a plain text (.txt) file. In this type of situation, if you want to do any kind of text analytics, you have to import plain text data into the R environment. In this recipe, you will import plain text data from a .txt file and store it into an object of class text.

Getting ready

Suppose you have stored a text file containing a newspaper article or several abstracts related to a particular topic. In this example, you will use a text file that contains 10 abstracts retrieved from PubMed by doing a literature search with the keyword term "Deep Learning". The filename is deapLearning.txt.

How to do it...

Importing plain text data from a .txt file is rather easy. It is like importing data from a CSV file. The only difference is that the resultant object will not be a data frame, rather it will be a vector of characters. Here is the single line of code to import text data from a .txt file:

```
absText <- readLines("deepLearning.txt")
```

How it works...

The `readLines()` function imports data line by line. If you have created the `.txt` file manually by typing the text content, then the number of lines will be the value equal to the number of times you pressed the *Enter* key on the keyboard. Alternatively, if the text sequence is too long and you didn't press the *Enter* key from the keyboard, then it will take the maximum possible number of characters in a single line before it breaks into a second line.

In this example, the `deepLearning.txt` file contains 10 abstracts, each representing a single line. The resultant object `absText` has a length of `10` because all of the abstract's text is stored in a single line of the file.

Here is the first element of the output character vector:

```
> absText[1]
[1] "Although deep learning approaches have had tremendous success
in image, video and audio processing, computer vision, and speech
recognition, their applications to three-dimensional (3D)
biomolecular structural data sets have been hindered by the
geometric and biological complexity. To address this problem we
introduce the element-specific persistent homology (ESPH) method.
ESPH represents 3D complex geometry by one-dimensional (1D)
topological invariants and retains important biological information
via a multichannel image-like representation. This representation
reveals hidden structure-function relationships in biomolecules. We
further integrate ESPH and deep convolutional neural networks to
construct a multichannel topological neural network (TopologyNet)
for the predictions of protein-ligand binding affinities and
protein stability changes upon mutation. To overcome the deep
learning limitations from small and noisy training sets, we propose
a multi-task multichannel topologic... <truncated>
```

There's more...

The plain text file comes with different encoding. The default encoding is "unknown", but if you have other encoding and you want to read the text data using your preferred encoding, then you can specify inside the `readLines()` function as follows:

```
absText <- readLines("deepLearning.txt", encoding="UTF-8")
```

Importing plain text data from a PDF file

The source text data could come in a portable document format (`.pdf`). Scientific research papers usually comes in PDF format. If you want to perform text mining, then you need to import the text from the PDF file into the R environment before doing any processing. In this recipe, you will import text data from a PDF file.

Getting ready

To implement this recipe, you will need to install the `pdftools` library.

To install the required library, run the following code:

```
install.packages("pdftools")
```

The source data for this recipe is given in the following three different PDF files containing three abstracts. The filenames are as follows:

- `abstract_1.pdf`
- `abstract_2.pdf`
- `abstract_3.pdf`

How to do it...

Let's take a look at the following steps to import plain text data from a PDF file:

1. Since you will read multiple PDF files, it is good to create an object containing all filenames. You can do this either by manually creating the object of filenames, or you can automatically read the filenames that have the PDF extension. Here is the code to automatically read the filenames:

```
pdfFileNames <- list.files(pattern = "pdf$")
```

2. Before running the preceding line, make sure that you have set your working directory using the `setwd()` function.

3. Once you have the list of filenames, you need to load the `pdftools` library into the R environment as follows:

```
library(pdftools)
```

4. Now you are ready to read the text data from the PDF file. Run the following code to get the text from all three PDF files:

```
txt <- sapply(pdfFileNames, pdf_text)
```

The newly created object `txt` contains a named character vector of the text imported from the PDF files. Here, the `spply()` function has been used to parse all PDF files into a single line of code.

How it works...

The PDF file stores the text in different layers, and the `pdf_text()` function reaches out to those layers and imports the relevant text data into the R environment. In this example, you supplied the PDF files that contain only plain text. Using this same function, you can extract bookmarks from the PDF if there are any.

If you are interested in extracting the meta data of a PDF file, such as font name, author name, version, and so on, then you can use the following intuitive functions:

```
> pdf_fonts(pdfFileNames[1])
            name       type embedded file
1 ELGFYK+Calibri truetype      TRUE

> info <- pdf_info(pdfFileNames[1])
> names(info)
[1] "version"      "pages"        "encrypted"   "linearized"  "keys"
"created"      "modified"
[8] "metadata"     "locked"       "attachments" "layout"
```

There's more...

There is another way to read a PDF file into the R environment. The `tm` library has a wrapper function called `readPDF()`. This function actually does not read the PDF document, rather it creates a function to read the PDF document. The typical structure of the `readPDF()` wrapper function is as follows:

```
readPDF(engine, control=list())
```

For more details on this function, you are directed to the documentation of the `readPDF()` function from the `tm` library.

Pre-processing text data for topic modeling and sentiment analysis

Sentiment analysis and topic modeling are one of the important applications of text mining. Also, in the medical field, biomedical text mining plays an important role in discovering new drugs, side effect, and much more. Before performing the analysis, it is obvious to do pre-processing of the text data. In this recipe, you will learn to do pre-processing to prepare the text data for text mining applications.

Getting ready

Suppose you want to perform topic modeling of the abstract extracted from PubMed by doing a literature search using "Deep Learning" as `keyword`. The objective is to see what the possible topics and subject areas are where the deep learning approach has been used. In this recipe, your ultimate task is to search the literature through PubMed, extract the abstract, and finally do the pre-processing. The search keyword is "Deep Learning". Also, your search will be restricted to the first 50 abstracts.

Here are the required libraries for this recipe:

- pubmed.mineR
- RISmed

If you don't have these libraries already installed on your computer, then run the following code to install them:

```
install.packages(c("pubmed.mineR", "RISmed"), dependencies = TRUE)
```

How to do it...

The whole process involves the following specific tasks:

1. Specify the search `keyword`.
2. Create PubMed `search_query` from the keyword.
3. Perform the search and limit it to the first 50 articles.
4. Extract the abstract texts and store them in an object.

   Here is the code to do the preceding task:

   ```
   library(pubmed.mineR)
   library(RISmed)
   keyword <- "Deep Learning"
   search_query <- EUtilsSummary(keyword, retmax=50)
   summary(search_query)
   extractedResult <- EUtilsGet(search_query)
   pmid <- PMID(extractedResult)
   years <- YearPubmed(extractedResult)
   Jtitle <- Title(extractedResult)
   articleTitle <- ArticleTitle(extractedResult)
   abstracts <- AbstractText(extractedResult)
   ```

Once you have the abstracts in your R session, the next step is to do the pre-processing of the texts. Here are the steps for pre-processing:

1. Convert all texts to either lowercase or uppercase.
2. Remove punctuation from the text.
3. Remove digits from the text.
4. Remove stop words.
5. Stemming the words, finding the root of a word or synonyms.
6. Before implementing the tasks, you should create a corpus of the text data. The whole process is implemented using the function available in the `tm` library:

   ```
   library(tm)
   AbstractCorpus <- Corpus(VectorSource(abstracts))
   AbstractCorpus <- tm_map(AbstractCorpus, content_transformer
   (tolower))
   AbstractCorpus <- tm_map(AbstractCorpus, removePunctuation)
   AbstractCorpus <- tm_map(AbstractCorpus, removeNumbers)
   Stopwords <- c(stopwords('english'))
   AbstractCorpus <- tm_map(AbstractCorpus, removeWords,
   Stopwords)
   AbstractCorpus <- tm_map(AbstractCorpus, stemDocument)
   ```

7. Once you have done all the initial processing, the final step is to create a term document matrix. This is a big sparse matrix. Whether a word is present in a document or not is indicated by a 1 or 0. To get the term document matrix, run the following code:

```
trmDocMat <- TermDocumentMatrix(AbstractCorpus, control =
list(minWordLength = 1))
```

How it works...

Let's take a look at the preceding process sequentially:

1. The initial phase was doing the PubMed search through the `pubmed.mineR` library.
2. The search `keyword` is converted into the PubMed `search_query` term using the `EUtilsSummary()` function.
3. Once the `search_query` term has been created, it parses through `EUtilsGet()` to get the actual search result from PubMed. The search results are extracted into an object.
4. Later on, the abstract text has been retrieved, and a vector has been created.
5. Once the vector of the text data has been created, the pre-processing step began from here. Using the `tm` library, you have created the corpus of the abstract by giving the vector input by the following code line:

```
AbstractCorpus <- Corpus(VectorSource(abstracts))
```

6. After creating the corpus, you are ready to apply other functions from the `tm` library to do further processing such as converting the text to lowercase or uppercase, removing numbers, removing punctuation, removing stop words, and stemming the document. The `tm_map()` function has intuitive options to perform all of these tasks. For example, to remove numbers, use the following code:

```
AbstractCorpus <- tm_map(AbstractCorpus, removeNumbers)
```

7. After doing all the necessary pre-processing, the final task is to create a term document matrix. This term document matrix is then used in topic modeling and sentiment analysis:

```
> trmDocMat
<<TermDocumentMatrix (terms: 1922, documents: 50)>>
Non-/sparse entries: 4500/91600
```

```
Sparsity            : 95%
Maximal term length: 28
Weighting           : term frequency (tf)
```

There's more...

The initial pre-processing can be done using regular expressions and without using the `tm` library. To learn more about the use of regular expressions, follow the *Using regular expression in text processing* recipe later in this chapter.

Creating a word cloud to explore unstructured text data

A word cloud is a visualization of text data where the actual words are displayed and the size of the word is determined by the frequency of the word into the whole corpus. This is one of the easy ways to understand the term frequency in a corpus of documents. Though in this recipe, you will learn to create a word cloud and explain it for general audience.

Getting ready

To implement this recipe, you will require a corpus of documents and the `wordcloud` library. First, install the `wordcloud` library by running the following code:

```
install.packages("wordcloud", dependencies = TRUE)
```

Since you will require a corpus of documents, let's create the corpus by doing the search through PubMed with the key `"Deep Learning"`. You will need the following libraries to create the corpus:

- `pubmed.mineR`
- `RISmed`
- `tm`

How to do it...

Let's perform the following steps to create a word cloud:

1. Perform a literature search through PubMed and the retrieve abstract texts.
2. Perform pre-processing using the `tm` library.
3. Create a term document matrix.
4. Create a word cloud.

The preceding steps are implemented as follows:

```
library(pubmed.mineR)
library(RISmed)
keyword <- "Deep Learning"
search_query <- EUtilsSummary(keyword, retmax=50)
summary(search_query)
extractedResult <- EUtilsGet(search_query)
pmid <- PMID(extractedResult)
years <- YearPubmed(extractedResult)
Jtitle <- Title(extractedResult)
articleTitle <- ArticleTitle(extractedResult)
abstracts <- AbstractText(extractedResult)
library(tm)
AbstractCorpus <- Corpus(VectorSource(abstracts))
AbstractCorpus <- tm_map(AbstractCorpus,
content_transformer(tolower))
AbstractCorpus <- tm_map(AbstractCorpus, removePunctuation)
AbstractCorpus <- tm_map(AbstractCorpus, removeNumbers)
Stopwords <- c(stopwords('english'))
AbstractCorpus <- tm_map(AbstractCorpus, removeWords,
Stopwords)
AbstractCorpus <- tm_map(AbstractCorpus, stemDocument)
trmDocMat <- TermDocumentMatrix(AbstractCorpus, control =
list(minWordLength = 1))
```

5. Now, you have the term document matrix. The next step is to create the word cloud visualization. To create the word cloud, the first thing you need is the frequency of each term in the whole corpus. You can achieve this task easily by taking the row sum of the term document matrix. Here is the code to calculate the frequency of each term in the whole corpus:

```
tdmMatrix <- as.matrix(trmDocMat)
freq <- sort(rowSums(tdmMatrix),decreasing=TRUE)
tdmDat <- data.frame(word = names(freq),freq=freq)
rownames(tdmDat) <- NULL
```

6. Finally, the word cloud has been created using the following code:

```
library(wordcloud)
wordcloud(tdmDat$word,tdmDat$freq,rot.per=.15,min.freq=10)
```

How it works...

A word cloud is one of the more popular ways to do exploratory text analysis. This is very intuitive and easy to understand. The first thing you need is a corpus of documents, and then, you need to do the pre-processing task such as converting all words into lowercase or uppercase, removing punctuation, and stopping words. The stemming also has been done to find the out root of a word. All of this pre-processing has been done using the functions available into the `tm` library.

After completing the pre-processing, the important step is to calculate term frequency from the term document matrix. Since the term document matrix is a sparse matrix with only 0 and 1 indicating whether a term is absent or present in the corpus, taking row sum of the matrix will give you the term frequency. The following code has been used to calculate term frequency:

```
tdmMatrix <- as.matrix(trmDocMat)
freq <- sort(rowSums(tdmMatrix),decreasing=TRUE)
tdmDat <- data.frame(word = names(freq),freq=freq)
rownames(tdmDat) <- NULL
```

Finally, the word cloud has the function to create the visualization as follows:

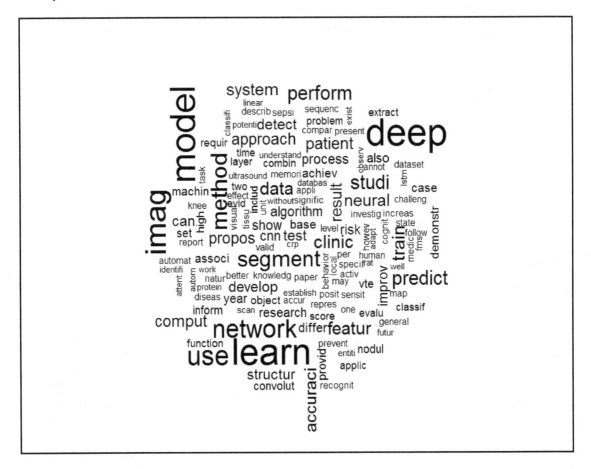

There's more...

The most basic code structure for a word cloud is as follows:

```
wordcloud(vector_of_word, vector_of_frequencies, minimum_frequency)
```

This code will create a basic black-and-white word cloud, but if you want to create a color visualization and the color comes from different sources, then you can specify using the color parameter. There are various other options available in the word cloud function. By typing help(wordcloud), you will be able to explore this further.

Using regular expression in text processing

A regular expression is simply a sequence of character strings that defines the search pattern. In natural language, processing and text mining are the two areas where regular expressions are used a lot. There are other application areas as well. In this recipe, you will perform text data pre-processing without using the tm library but by using a regular expression.

Getting ready

Suppose you have a corpus of documents and your objective is to find the frequent words in the corpus. So, the first thing is to do the pre-processing and then create term a document matrix. In this recipe, you will use a regular expression on the text data retrieved from a web page using the readLines() function. Specifically, you will read the following web page using the readLines() function:

```
https://en.wikipedia.org/wiki/Programming_with_Big_Data_in_R
```

How to do it...

Let's take a look at the following steps to learn how to use a regular expression in text processing:

1. To read the text from an URL, first, you need to create a connection between your R session and the web page.
2. Note that your computer must be connected to the internet to run this recipe. Once you have connected and created the connection of R session, you are ready to retrieve the HTML code form of the page. Here is the code to do the whole thing:

```
sourceURL <-
"https://en.wikipedia.org/wiki/Programming_with_Big_Data_in_R"
link2web <- url(sourceURL)
htmlText <- readLines(link2web)
close(link2web)
```

3. Now you have the HTML text in an object called `htmlText`. This object contains plain text as well as HTML tag pairs. The task is to remove all HTML tags, punctuation, and numbers using a regular expression as follows:

```
# Remove html tags
htmlText = gsub("<.*?>", "", htmlText)
# remove puntuation
htmlText = gsub("[[:punct:]]", " ", htmlText)
# remove numbers
htmlText <- gsub('\\d+', '', htmlText)
```

How it works...

Let's take a look at the following process sequentially:

1. The `url()` function takes a character string as an input and creates a connection between the web page and the R session.

2. After establishing the connection, you can read each line of the HTML source code of the page. The output will be a vector of character strings. This output contains HTML tags, punctuation, numbers, and so on. Here is the partial output of the HTML source code extracted from the link:

```
> htmlText[1:6]
[1] "<!DOCTYPE html>"
[2] "<html class=\"client-nojs\" lang=\"en\" dir=\"ltr\">"
[3] "<head>"
[4] "<meta charset=\"UTF-8\"/>"
[5] "<title>Programming with Big Data in R - Wikipedia</title>"
[6] "<script>document.documentElement.className =
document.documentElement.className.replace( /(^|\\s)client-
nojs(\\s|$)/, \"$1client-js$2\" );</script>"
```

3. Now, to remove the HTML tags, the regular expression will be `"<*?>"`. You need to parse this expression into the `gsub` function and replace the tag pair with a blank. The exact code is as follows:

```
htmlText = gsub("<.*?>", "", htmlText)
```

After running the preceding code, you will have the following output:

```
> htmlText[1:6]
[1] ""
[2] ""
[3] ""
[4] ""
[5] "Programming with Big Data in R - Wikipedia"
[6] "document.documentElement.className =
document.documentElement.className.replace( /(^|\\s)client-
nojs(\\s|$)/, \"$1client-js$2\" );"
```

4. You will notice that there is not HTML tags are there into this new output. But there is punctuation available. The next thing is to remove that punctuation with the following code:

```
> htmlText[1:6]
[1] ""
[2] ""
[3] ""
[4] ""
[5] "Programming with Big Data in R   Wikipedia"
[6] "document documentElement className   document
documentElement className replace        s client nojs   s
1client js 2      "
```

5. Finally, the numbers have been removed using the following code snippet:

```
> htmlText[1:6]
[1] ""
[2] ""
[3] ""
[4] ""
[5] "Programming with Big Data in R   Wikipedia"
[6] "document documentElement className   document
documentElement className replace        s client nojs   s
client js       "
```

There's more...

In this recipe, you have seen a few examples of regular expressions, but there are a lot of regular expressions that can be used within the `gsub()` function to perform text processing. There are libraries available in R that use regular expressions to develop string processing functions such as `stringr`, `stringi`, and `regex`. Moreover, `grep()` is also able to do text processing using regular expressions.

8
R and Databases

The smaller datasets can be stored in a flat file like the conventional CSV file. However, whenever we encounter larger datasets and there are multiple datasets with an inherent relationship between them, it is good to store those types of data in database management software. Using R, you can easily interact with larger datasets through a connection between R session and the database management software. In this chapter, the following recipes will walk you through the process of interacting with database management software from within R:

- Installing the PostgreSQL database server
- Creating a new user in the PostgreSQL database server
- Creating a table in a database in PostgreSQL
- Creating a dataset in PostgreSQL from R
- Interacting with the PostgreSQL database from R
- Creating and interacting with the SQLite database from R

Introduction

A database management system is a software to store, process, and upload data into a computer system. The database management system is usually used for managing larger datasets and the relational data. The relational database contains multiple data tables with a defined relation between tables, using some key variables known as the primary key and secondary key. In the database management software, they should have a primary key to uniquely identify a single row from a data table. There are a lots of database management software available, ranging from open source (free) to Enterprise Edition (commercial) versions.

The most commonly used database management software are Microsoft SQL Server, MySQL, PostgreSQL, Oracle, and so on. The open source community mostly uses PostgreSQL and MySQL because these two are easy to use and freely available. In this chapter, you will use PostgreSQL from within R to interact with datasets.

Also, to interact with various database management systems, R has the capability to connect with the database through **Open Database Connectivity** (**ODBC**). You will also go through ODBC and learn how to work from R with ODBC. In the end, you will see how you can use an SQL statement for working with a dataset in the R environment.

Installing the PostgreSQL database server

PostgreSQL is one of the most powerful database management systems, and is publicly available, and free of cost. This open source database management software runs on every platform, including Windows, Linux, and macOS. Using this database management system, you will be able to store and process very large data. The following table will give you an understanding of how large data can be handled using the PostgreSQL database:

Limit	Value
Maximum database size	Unlimited
Maximum table size	32 TB
Maximum row size	1.6 TB
Maximum field size	1 GB
Maximum row per table	Unlimited
Maximum columns per table	250-1,600 depending on column types
Maximum indexes per table	Unlimited

Capacity of PostgreSQL database (source: `https://www.postgresql.org/about/`)

In this recipe, you will download and install PostgreSQL onto your computer. This recipe is based on the Windows operating system, specifically Windows 7 64-bit.

Getting ready

To download the installer file, visit the PostgreSQL official website (`https://www.postgresql.org/`) and then perform the following steps:

1. Once you are in the home page of the PostgreSQL official website, go to the **Download** page.
2. On this page, you will see the options for various operating systems. Click on **Windows**.
3. On the **Windows** download page, click on **Download the installer** under the **Interactive installer by EnterpriseDB** section.
4. Once you click there, it will redirect you to another page where you will be given the option to select the specific operating system and the version of PostgreSQL. Then, hit the **DOWNLOAD NOW** button.

The installer will be downloaded onto your computer, and you are ready to install it.

How to do it...

Let's perform the following steps to install the PostgreSQL database server:

1. Since you have downloaded the installer file, you can simply double-click on the file, and it will initiate the installation wizard as shown in the following screenshot:

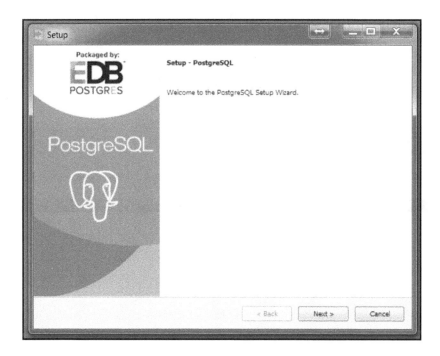

2. At this stage, the most obvious thing is to click on the **Next >** button to proceed with the installation. After you click on the **Next >** button, it will take you to another screen asking for the location where you want to store all of the installation files. The default location will be inside the `Program Files` directory, but you can change this based on your convenience:

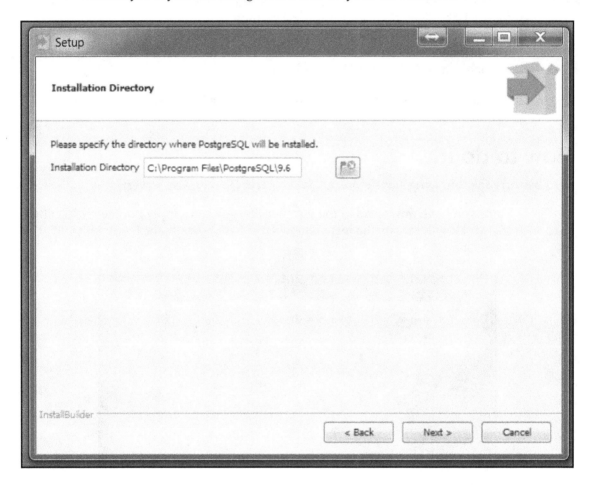

3. After selecting the installation directory, again click on **Next >**. It will then take you to another screen where you will be asked to select a directory to store your data. Use a convenient location to store the data and then click on **Next >**:

4. Now, you will be asked to provide a password for your database for the super user (`postgres`). You must remember this password because you need it to get access to the database server and create new users. For convenience, let's use `postgres123` as the password, as shown in the following screenshot:

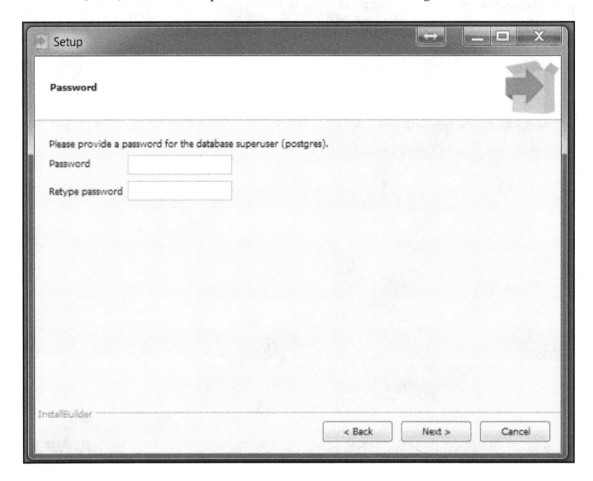

5. After giving the password, click on **Next >**. It will take you to another screen asking for the port number to access the database. The default port is 5432. You can keep the default port number or you can use another one. For the time being, let's keep the default one and click on **Next >**:

6. Now, at this stage, you will be asked to select the installation language; keep this default locale, and proceed by clicking on **Next >**. Finally, it is ready to install:

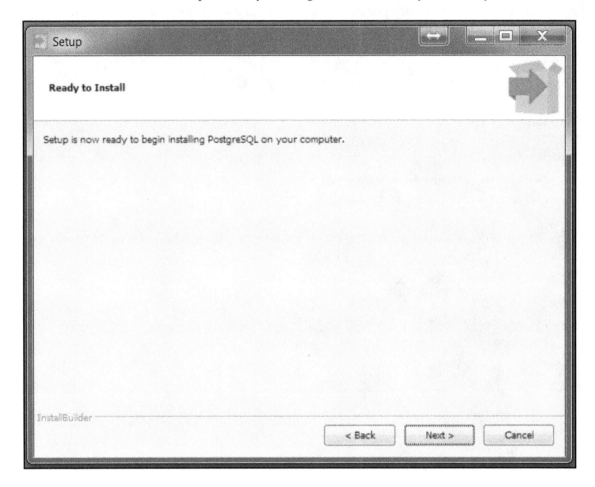

7. After finishing the installation, you will see the screen as shown in the following screenshot for installing additional tools (if you want). At this stage, deselect the **Stack Builder may be used to download and install additional tools, drivers and applications to complement your PostgreSQL installation.** option and safely click on **Finish**. You have successfully completed the installation part of the PostgreSQL database onto your computer:

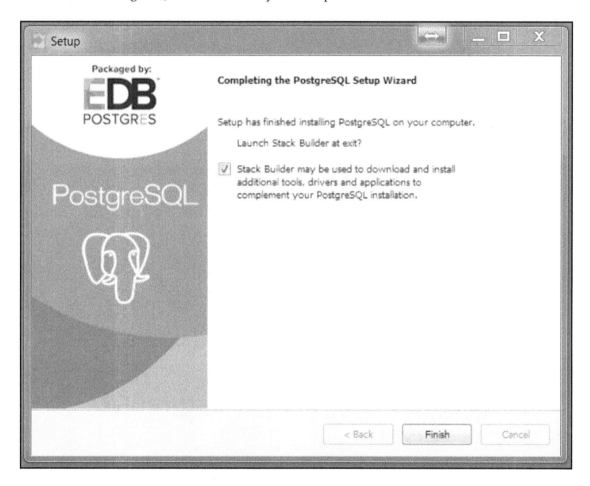

How it works...

Since this is a database server, after completing installation, it will run in the background. The installation steps are intuitive and easily understandable. The question is how to check whether it is installed correctly or not. Let's check by performing the following few steps:

1. To check the installation, go to the **Start** menu of your computer and then select PostgreSQK 9.6 from the programs. Then, open pgAdmin 4. This is a user interface to the PostgreSQL database.

2. Once you try to open pgAdmin 4, it will ask you the password that you gave during installation, as shown in the following screenshot:

Creating a new user in the PostgreSQL database server

In every database server, there should be one database administrator and many user clients. The administrator creates new users and defines roles for each user. Once you have installed the PostgreSQL onto your computer, the super user administrator will have been automatically defined under the postgres username. Now, you can create a new user using the postgres account. In this recipe, you will create a new user and define its role.

Getting ready

It is always good to create a new user and log in using the new user to create a database. In that case, you will always be in a safe situation, and you can easily avoid accidental damage to your database server. In this recipe, you will create a new user, say `testuser`, with the following initial privilege:

- The new user can create a database
- The new user cannot create/modify the role of another user

How to do it...

To create a new user in the PostgreSQL database server, perform the following steps:

1. Open Command Prompt by typing `cmd` into the Windows **Start** menu search box.
2. Navigate to the installation directory where you have installed PostgreSQL. More precisely, navigate to the `bin` folder within the PostgreSQL installation directory, as shown in the following screenshot:

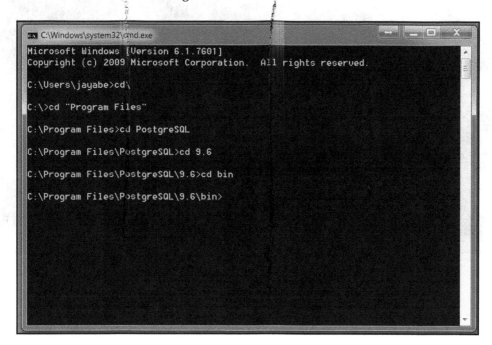

3. Now, to create a new user `testuser`, execute the following command:

```
createuser.exe --createdb --username postgres --no-createrole
--pwprompt testuser
```

4. Once you enter the preceding command, it will ask you to type a new password for the `testuser` user. Let's say you are giving a new password `testuser123`. After typing the password, it will ask you to re-type, and finally, it will ask for you to enter the password again. At this stage, enter the password that you have used for the `postgres` user, `postgres123`. After completing the process, you will see the following screenshot:

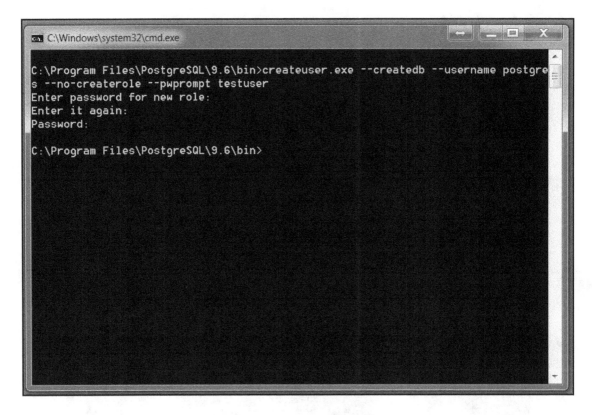

5. Now, you can log in to the **pgAdmin 4** dashboard to see the newly created user. It will show a screen similar to the following screenshot:

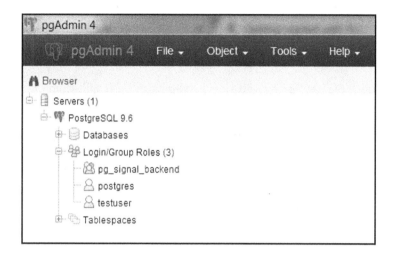

You can see that the new username is on the list under the `Login/Group Roles` directory.

How it works...

In the `bin` folder under PostgreSQL installation directory, there is one executable file called `createuser.exe`. This file has been used for creating the new user account in the database server. The explanation for each part of the code is given as follows:

- `--createdb`: This command has been used to give permission to create a new database by the newly created user
- `--username`: This command has been used to specify the user account used to create the new user in the database
- `--no-createrole`: This command has been used to suppress the newly created user to creating/modifying the role for other users
- `--pwprompt`: This command has been used for assigning a new password for the newly created user

During the user creation, there is no instant feedback in Command Prompt. If every command is correctly given, then it will return to the prompt without any error.

There's more...

After creating the new user from Command Prompt, you can modify the role of the new user from the **pgAdmin 4** dashboard by performing the following steps:

1. To do so, log in using the postgres user ID and then go to the new user testuser under Login/Group Roles.

2. Right-click on testuser and select **Properties...**. It will then open the properties window as shown in the following screenshot:

3. You can modify the privilege of the `testuser` user from this window by going to the **Privileges** tab of this window. Moreover, you can set an expiry date for the new account from the **Definition** tab.

See also

To know more about PostgreSQL, visit the official documentation page at `https://www.postgresql.org/docs/`.

Creating a table in a database in PostgreSQL

A database is a structured set of data with one or multiple numbers of tables in it to store, query, create, or perform any other kind of processing. Once you have installed the database software such as PostgreSQL onto your computer, the next obvious task is to create a database and then insert tables (actual data) into that database. In this recipe, you will create a database in the PostgreSQL database server.

Getting ready

Before creating a data table, you should connect with the database server, and it should run properly onto your computer. The task is to create a new data table called `airlinesDB`. The data table will contain the following columns:

- `YEAR` (**integer**)
- `QUARTER` (**integer**)
- `MONTH` (**integer**)
- `ORIGIN` (**character**, 3)
- `DEST` (**character**, 3)
- `DEP_DELAY` (**numeric**, 6 digits with 2 decimals)
- `ARR_DELAY` (**numeric**, 6 digits with 2 decimals)

How to do it...

The easiest way to create a data table in the PostgreSQL database server is to use pgAdmin 4. Connect to the database server using the user ID that you will use to create the data table. In this case, you will log in using the `postgres` ID. Once you are connected to the database, perform the following steps:

1. Expand the **Databases** lists.
2. Expand **Schemas**.
3. Expand **public**.
4. Right-click on **Tables**. Then, select **Create** and click on **Table...**.

Now, you have the **Create - Table** dialogue box opened as shown in the following screenshot:

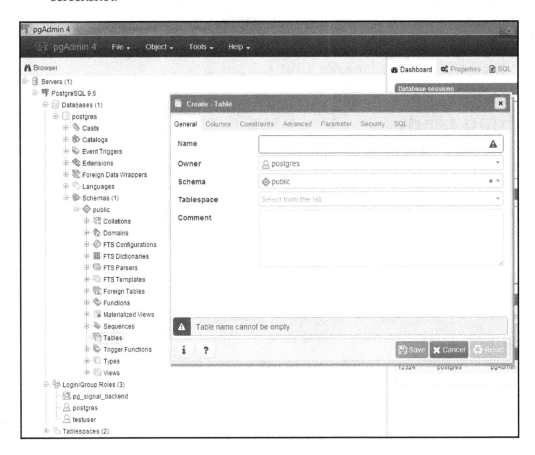

5. In this box, the first step is to give the data table name as `airlineDB`. After giving the name, the next step is to define each of the columns as per their properties, as shown in the following screenshot:

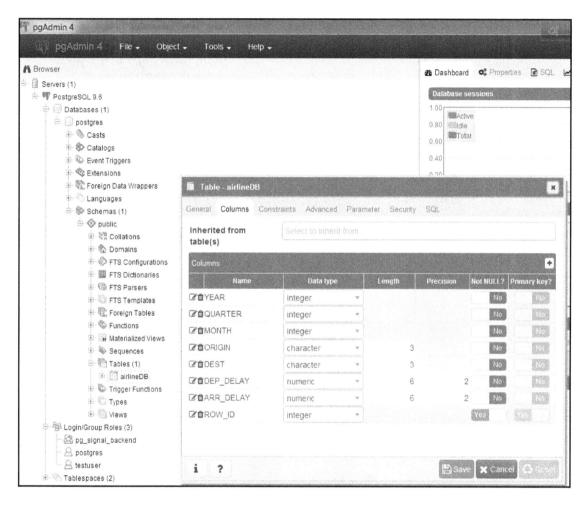

Here, `ROW_ID` is a unique serial number for each row. It will be used as a primary key for this database.

How it works...

The data table is now ready under the `postgres` database. The steps described in the previous section are quite intuitive. After opening the **Create - Table** dialogue box, the obvious step is to give the table name. After that, explicitly define each of the columns with their properties. In this case, there were four integer variables, two character variables, and two numeric variables. Since each data table should have one primary key to uniquely identify each row, the `ROW_ID` column has been added to serve this purpose.

There's more...

After creating the data table, you are ready to import data from external sources. If you already imported the data, then you can view the data here. Just right-click on the data table name. Then, there will be a submenu for performing several tasks, as shown in the following screenshot:

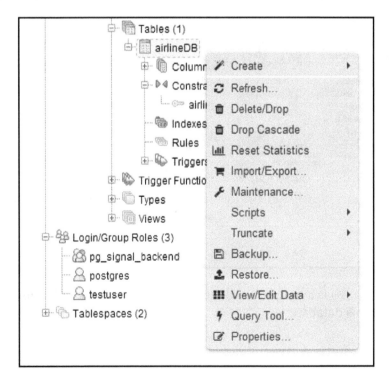

Creating a dataset in PostgreSQL from R

The PostgreSQL database server can be accessed from R through the RPostgreSQL library. You can either create a new database, insert data into an existing database, or perform queries on the existing data tables. In this recipe, you will connect R with the PostgreSQL database server and create a table under the postgres database, and insert data into the database.

Getting ready

To connect with the PostgreSQL database server from R, you are required to install the RPostgreSQL library along with its dependencies. The following R code is to used install the necessary libraries to access the PostgreSQL database:

```
install.packages("RPostgreSQL", dependencies = TRUE)
```

In this recipe, the USAairlineData2016.csv file has been used as a raw data source. You will insert the subset of this dataset into postgres in the PostgreSQL database. The airlineDB table will be created using R.

 Note that postgres is the default database under the super user postgres.

How to do it...

To connect with the PostgreSQL database server, you need to know the username and password. Here is the R code to connect to the database server, create a database, and insert the data into it:

```
library(RPostgreSQL)
p_word <- {
  "postgres123"
}

databaseDriver <- dbDriver("PostgreSQL")
con2DB <- dbConnect(databaseDriver, dbname = "postgres",
 host = "localhost", port = 5432,
 user = "postgres", password = p_word)
dbExistsTable(con2DB, "airlineDB")
```

```
# Importing CSV file
dat1 <- read.csv('USAairlineData2016.csv', header = T, as.is = T)
dat1 <- dat1[c("YEAR", "QUARTER", "MONTH", "ORIGIN", "DEST",
"DEP_DELAY", "ARR_DELAY")]
dat1$ROW_ID <- 1:nrow(dat1)

# Writing the data into PostgreSQL data table "airlineDB"
dbWriteTable(con2DB, "airlineDB",
value = dat1, append = TRUE, row.names = FALSE)
dat2 <- dbGetQuery(con2DB, 'SELECT * FROM "airlineDB"')

# disconnect the connection to server
dbDisconnect(con2DB)

# disconnect driver
dbUnloadDriver(databaseDriver)
```

How it works...

Every database software has its own driver that helps it to connect with the database.

Let's take a look at the following steps and see how they work:

1. The first step to connect with the PostgreSQL database server is to call the driver and then connect with it. The following line of R code is used to activate the PostgreSQL database driver into R session:

   ```
   databaseDriver <- dbDriver("PostgreSQL")
   ```

2. Once the driver is activated, the next task is to create a connection string with the database server and R session with the following code:

   ```
   con2DB <- dbConnect(databaseDriver, dbname = "postgres",  host
   = "localhost", port = 5432, user = "postgres", password =
   p_word)
   ```

3. The dbConnect() function takes the driver object as the first argument, and then all the other necessary information. In this case, dbname is the database name that you are intending to connect with, and postgres is the default database. The host and port arguments are the address of the database server used to gain access. You also need to supply the username and password to get connected. In this example, the super user postgres has been used. After running the preceding code line, you are ready to insert the data table into the database.

In this chapter, in the *Creating a table in a database in PostgreSQL* recipe, you had created a table called `airlineDB`. You are going to insert data into this table.

The following line is to check whether the table `airlineDB` exists in the `postgres` database:

```
dbExistsTable(con2DB, "airlineDB")
[1] TRUE
```

4. Once the result of this line is `TRUE`, you are finally ready to insert the data. Now, read the `USAairlineData2016.csv` file into R and keep only the necessary variables. Then, create a new column `ROW_ID`. This is just a serial number starting from 1:

```
dat1 <- read.csv('USAairlineData2016.csv', header = T, as.is = T)
dat1 <- dat1[c("YEAR", "QUARTER", "MONTH", "ORIGIN", "DEST",
"DEP_DELAY", "ARR_DELAY")]
dat1$ROW_ID <- 1:nrow(dat1)
head(dat1)

# The first 6 rows of the dataset
> head(dat1)
  YEAR QUARTER MONTH ORIGIN DEST DEP_DELAY ARR_DELAY ROW_ID
1 2016       1     1    DTW  LAX         0       -24      1
2 2016       1     1    ATL  GRR         5        -2      2
3 2016       1     1    LAX  ATL         1       -13      3
4 2016       1     1    SLC  ATL         4       -16      4
5 2016       1     1    BZN  MSP        72       124      5
6 2016       1     1    ATL  BNA        83        83      6
```

The following line takes `dat1` as input and inserts the entire dataset into the PostgreSQL data table `airlineDB`:

```
dbWriteTable(con2DB, "airlineDB", value = dat1, append = TRUE,
row.names = FALSE)
```

5. To check whether the data has been correctly inserted into the database, you can retrieve the dataset from another object called `dat2` using the following code snippet:

```
dat2 <- dbGetQuery(con2DB, 'SELECT * FROM "airlineDB"')
head(dat2)

# First six rows of the dataset retrieved from database
> head(dat2)
  YEAR QUARTER MONTH ORIGIN DEST DEP_DELAY ARR_DELAY ROW_ID
```

1	2016	1	1	DTW	LAX	0	-24	1
2	2016	1	1	ATL	GRR	5	-2	2
3	2016	1	1	LAX	ATL	1	-13	3
4	2016	1	1	SLC	ATL	4	-16	4
5	2016	1	1	BZN	MSP	72	124	5
6	2016	1	1	ATL	BNA	83	83	6

6. Finally, disconnect the database driver and the connection to the server by executing the following code:

```
dbDisconnect(con2DB)
dbUnloadDriver(databaseDriver)
```

Interacting with the PostgreSQL database from R

A dataset is not only used for storing information, but, usually, you also need to interact with it to find out useful information. Whenever the dataset has been stored in a database, the interactive process is more efficient in terms of memory and processing time. In this recipe, you will interact with a data table that has already been stored in a database in the PostgreSQL database server.

Getting ready

Let's consider that you have created a database postgres and stored a dataset in it with the table name airlineDB. To get access to the database server, you will require the username and password for the owner of the database. Here is the username and password for the database:

- **Username:** postgres
- **Password:** postres123

The dataset that has been stored under the postgres database is the airlineDB table, and it contains the following columns:

- YEAR (**integer**)
- QUARTER (**integer**)
- MONTH (**integer**)

- ORIGIN (**character**, 3)
- DEST (**character**, 3)
- DEP_DELAY (**numeric**, 6 digits with 2 decimals)
- ARR_DELAY (**numeric**, 6 digits with 2 decimals)

The task in this recipe is to extract the following information from the database:

- Unique values of the ORIGIN column and associated frequencies
- Create a subset of the data by taking only those rows that have a negative value in the DEP_DELAY column
- Create a dataset containing the average value of the DEP_DELAY column for each value of the ORIGIN column

How to do it...

Here are the steps to accomplish the task listed in the *Getting ready* section of this recipe:

1. Establish a connection between R and the database server.
2. Parse the SQL statements for each task and retrieve the results.

   Here is the code to accomplish the preceding tasks:

   ```
   library(RPostgreSQL)
   databaseDriver <- dbDriver("PostgreSQL")
   con2DB <- dbConnect(databaseDriver, dbname = "postgres",
   host = "localhost", port = 5432, user = "postgres",
   password = "postgres123")
   uniqueOrigin <- dbGetQuery(con2DB, 'SELECT "ORIGIN", COUNT(*)
   AS freq FROM "airlineDB" GROUP BY "ORIGIN"')
   negDelay <- dbGetQuery(con2DB, 'SELECT * FROM "airlineDB" WHERE
   "DEP_DELAY"<0')
   avgDelay <- dbGetQuery(con2DB, 'SELECT "ORIGIN",
   avg("DEP_DELAY") AS avgDelay FROM "airlineDB" GROUP BY
   "ORIGIN"')
   ```

How it works...

To connect with the PostgreSQL server from R, the RPostgreSQL library is required, and this library has already been loaded in the first place. The dbDriver() function extracts the necessary database driver that needs to interact with the database from external software, such as R in this case. The dbConnect() function takes the database driver, username, password, and the host name along with the port number as the input and creates a connection between R session and the database server. Once the connection has been established, then you are ready to interact with the database.

To create a new R dataset by taking the unique value of the column named ORIGIN and the frequency of occurrence of each value of the ORIGIN column, the following code has been used:

```
uniqueOrigin <- dbGetQuery(con2DB, 'SELECT "ORIGIN", COUNT(*) AS
freq FROM "airlineDB" GROUP BY "ORIGIN"')

# the output of newly created object containing "ORIGIN" and its
frequency
> head(uniqueOrigin)
  ORIGIN  freq
1    ANC 17152
2    ELP 11213
3    CAE  4392
4    BNA 51118
5    IMT   672
6    SGF  2806
```

Take a look at the following code:

```
negDelay <- dbGetQuery(con2DB, 'SELECT * FROM "airlineDB" WHERE
"DEP_DELAY"<0')
```

Let's see the first few lines of the output:

```
> head(negDelay)
  YEAR QUARTER MONTH ORIGIN DEST DEP_DELAY ARR_DELAY ROW_ID
1 2016       1     1    JAX  ATL        -1       -15      9
2 2016       1     1    ATL  OKC        -3       -12     10
3 2016       1     1    MSP  SMF        -2       -33     11
4 2016       1     1    LAX  JFK        -7       -14     12
5 2016       1     1    ATL  MDT        -1       -11     13
6 2016       1     1    MDT  ATL       -10       -15     14
```

Notice that the dataset name (the table name in the database) should be kept inside quotations. Similar rules apply for the variable name too. After the SELECT keyword, the asterisk (*) indicates the need to keep all available variables from the data table where the value of the DEP_DELAY column is less than zero.

Finally, the output of average delay is as follows:

```
avgDelay <- dbGetQuery(con2DB, 'SELECT "ORIGIN", avg("DEP_DELAY")
AS avgDelay FROM "airlineDB" GROUP BY "ORIGIN"')
> head(avgDelay)
  ORIGIN    avgdelay
1    ANC  0.05393535
2    ELP  6.90984195
3    CAE 11.45416763
4    BNA  8.91835078
5    IMT  6.10334347
6    SGF  8.42473703
```

There's more...

Once you have a database and the data is stored in it, you can easily interact with it. The full range of SQL statements can be used using the dbGetQuery() function. The only thing you have to be careful of is the name of the table and the name of variables. You should use double quotations for both the table name and variable names. Moreover, the entire SQL statement should be enclosed with single quotations.

Creating and interacting with the SQLite database from R

The SQLite library implements serverless, self-contained, and zero-configuration database engines. Also, SQLite is publicly available free of cost. You can create, store, and interact with the SQLite database from R. In this recipe, you will create a new database in SQLite and insert a data table with the mtcars data from R.

Getting ready

To implement this recipe, you will need the following libraries installed onto your computer:

- RSQLite
- DBI
- sqldf

You can use the following code to install the RSQLite library with its necessary dependencies:

```
install.packages("RSQLite", dependencies = TRUE)
```

In this recipe, you will use the mtcars dataset from the datasets library. This is one of the well-known default datasets in R containing various characteristics of a car. Once the library installation is completed, you are ready to go.

The task is to create a new database called dbNew and then create a table cardata containing the mtcars dataset. Finally, extract a subset of the data by taking only automatic transmission cars with the variable "am" == 0.

How to do it...

The steps for this recipe are as as follows:

1. Load the RSQLite library.
2. Create an object by calling up the SQLite database driver.
3. Create a connection string with the database engine and R session. The database will be created in this same step.
4. Create a data table and insert actual data from the mtcars dataset.
5. Extract only those rows containing automatic transmission cars with the variable "am" ==0.
6. Display the first few rows of the extracted dataset.
7. Disconnect the database driver.
8. Disconnect the database.

The code to perform the preceding tasks is as follows:

```
library(RSQLite)
dbDriverSQLite <- dbDriver("SQLite")
dbNew <- dbConnect(drv = dbDriverSQLite, dbname="testdbSQL")
carTable <- dbWriteTable(con =  dbNew, name = "cardata", value
= mtcars)
dbListTables(dbNew)
autocars <- dbGetQuery(conn = dbNew, 'SELECT * FROM "cardata"
WHERE "am"==0')
head(autocars)
dbDisconnect(dbNew)
dbUnloadDriver(dbDriverSQLite)
```

How it works...

The dbConnect() function is used either to connect with an existing database or to create a new one if there aren't any. In this example, testdbSQL is a new database that has been created using the dbConnect() function. This function takes the database driver string as one of the inputs and then the name of the database. Once the database connection string has been created, you are ready to interact with the database.

After creating the database, the next thing is to create a data table and insert data into it. The following code line is to create a data table and insert actual data from the source data mtcars from the datasets library:

```
carTable <- dbWriteTable(con =  dbNew, name = "cardata", value =
mtcars)
```

You can check whether the table has been created or not by executing the following code line:

```
dbListTables(dbNew)
[1] "cardata"
```

Once you see that the new data table has been created, you can query from the table. The following line is to extract the rows with the column "am" ==0:

```
autocars <- dbGetQuery(conn = dbNew, 'SELECT * FROM "cardata" WHERE
"am"==0')
```

The output of the newly created subset of original the data is as follows:

```
> head(autocars)
         row_names  mpg cyl  disp  hp drat    wt  qsec vs am gear carb
1     Hornet 4 Drive 21.4   6 258.0 110 3.08 3.215 19.44  1  0    3    1
2 Hornet Sportabout 18.7   8 360.0 175 3.15 3.440 17.02  0  0    3    2
3           Valiant 18.1   6 225.0 105 2.76 3.460 20.22  1  0    3    1
4        Duster 360 14.3   8 360.0 245 3.21 3.570 15.84  0  0    3    4
5        Merc 240D 24.4   4 146.7  62 3.69 3.190 20.00  1  0    4    2
6          Merc 230 22.8   4 140.8  95 3.92 3.150 22.90  1  0    4    2
```

There's more...

In this recipe, you created a database in the SQLite database engine using the RSQLite library. You can do a similar thing using the sqldf library as well. To know more on this, you could follow https://www.r-bloggers.com/r-and-sqlite-part-1/ to view a Blog post on this topic.

9
Parallel Processing in R

In data science application development, such as credit card fraud detection, airline delay prediction, sentiment analysis from a huge corpus of text, and so on, we are required to store, process, and analyze a dataset that might not fit into computer memory. Moreover, in some situations, the dataset might not be that big but the complexity of the algorithm forces us to use huge memory. In these types of situations where the dataset is way too big, or the algorithm is too complex, you are required to use parallel processing to achieve the task. In R, the data frame is the most convenient and popular structure to store, process, and analyze a dataset, but for a larger data context, the data frame is not fast enough. The **external data frame** (**XDF**) is an alternative to the typical R data frame used to store, process, and analyze larger data. In this chapter, we will use the parallel processing approach to solve memory problems with a larger dataset, and we will use the XDF file for processing. Specifically, the following recipes will be covered in this chapter:

- Creating an XDF file from CSV input
- Processing data as a chunk
- Comparing computation time with data frame and XDF
- Linear regression with larger data (rxFastLiner)

Introduction

As a data scientist or data analyst, you often need to repeat certain computations or series of computations many times. To complete repetitive tasks you could easily use a `for` loop in R. But if you need a larger number of repetitions or a very complex computation, the `for` loop could a be time consuming. To overcome slow computation problems, you could use multiple computation cores that are available in any recent computer. You can easily spread your task to multiple computing cores in your computer to simplify complex and repetitive tasks.

Suppose you want to predict airline delay (departure delay) time for each destination, you could do this using simple regression, but for larger data and for each destination, this could be a computational problem and consume huge memory. You can tackle this computational issue by using parallel computing facilities available in R. There are several libraries to do parallel computing in R; the following are the most commonly used libraries:

- `parallel`
- `doMC`
- `foreach`
- `RevoScaleR`
- `MicrosoftML`

There are other libraries available performing parallel computing in R, but the preceding are the more popular libraries in this area. In this chapter, you will learn how to work with a dataset that does not fit into your computer memory (RAM), how to process a dataset chunk by chunk, and develop a Machine Learning model with a larger dataset.

Creating an XDF file from CSV input

An XDF file is a data file format in R used to store, process, and analyze a larger dataset. This file uses persistent memory, that is, hard disk storage, instead of RAM. The XDF file allows you to process datasets by chunks and takes less time than the typical R data frame. In this recipe, you will create a new XDF file from a CSV input file. The XDF file is not a primary choice for parallel processing, but it offers better control over your data through persisted storage and further processing.

Getting ready

To implement this recipe, you are required to install the `RevoScaleR` library.

The datasets (the CSV input files) used in this recipe are downloaded from the website of the Bureau of Transportation Statistics, USA (http://www.transtats.bts.gov). There are in total 12 CSV files for 12 months and they contains 61 variables. Your task is to import the CSV file and create an XDF file for processing.

To install `RevoScaleR`, you can run the following code:

```
install.packages("RevoScaleR", dependencies = T)
```

Note that to install the `RevoScaleR` library, you should have Microsoft R Client on your computer. Refer to the *Installing and configuring R tools for Visual Studio in Windows* recipe from `Chapter 1`, *Installing and Configuring R and its Libraries*.

How to do it...

The following are the steps to convert one or multiple CSV files into a single XDF file:

1. Set the working directory where the CSV file is stored.
2. Load the `RevoScaleR` library.
3. Extract the CSV filenames and store them in an object.
4. Create an object with the XDF filename.
5. Use the `rxImport()` function and pass each of the CSV files through it and create an XDF file by appending rows.

   Here's the code chunk for the preceding steps:

   ```
   setwd("D:/AllSync/Drive/Book-3/codeBundle/ch9")

   library(RevoScaleR)
   csvFiles <- dir(pattern = ".csv")

   xdfFile <- file.path(getwd(), "USAirlines2016.xdf")

   for(i in 1:length(csvFiles)){
     print(csvFiles[i])
     if(i!=1){
       rxImport(inData = csvFiles[i], outFile = xdfFile,
       overwrite = TRUE, append = "rows")
     }
     else {
       rxImport(inData = csvFiles[i], outFile = xdfFile)
     }
   }
   ```

How it works...

At the beginning, the `setwd()` function sets the data location for the R session. After that, using `dir()`, it extracts the name of the CSV files. This way you do not need to give the filename manually. Once you have the CSV filename stored in an object, you will be able to use that object later.

Make sure that you load the `RevoScaleR` library before calling the `rxImport()` function. Since you are working with 12 CSV files, you need a loop to call each CSV file through `rxImport()`. The first CSV file will then have converted into an XDF file and been stored in the `USAirline2016.xdf` file. The subsequent CSV file is then imported and appended into that same file.

When you run the `rxImport()` function, you will be able to see the following output by default:

```
[1] "2016_01.csv"
Rows Read: 445827, Total Rows Processed: 445827, Total
Chunk Time: 1.176 seconds
[1] "2016_02.csv"
Rows Read: 423889, Total Rows Processed: 423889, Total
Chunk Time: 1.109 seconds
[1] "2016_03.csv"
Rows Read: 423889, Total Rows Processed: 423889, Total
Chunk Time: 1.105 seconds
[1] "2016_04.csv"
Rows Read: 461630, Total Rows Processed: 461630, Total
Chunk Time: 1.177 seconds
[1] "2016_05.csv"
Rows Read: 479358, Total Rows Processed: 479358, Total
Chunk Time: 1.266 seconds
[1] "2016_06.csv"
Rows Read: 487637, Total Rows Processed: 487637, Total
Chunk Time: 1.293 seconds
[1] "2016_07.csv"
Rows Read: 502457, Total Rows Processed: 502457, Total
Chunk Time: 1.263 seconds
[1] "2016_08.csv"
Rows Read: 498347, Total Rows Processed: 498347, Total
Chunk Time: 1.256 seconds
[1] "2016_09.csv"
Rows Read: 454878, Total Rows Processed: 454878, Total
Chunk Time: 1.143 seconds
[1] "2016_10.csv"
Rows Read: 472626, Total Rows Processed: 472626, Total
Chunk Time: 1.223 seconds
```

```
[1] "2016_11.csv"
Rows Read: 450938, Total Rows Processed: 450938, Total
Chunk Time: 1.239 seconds
[1] "2016_12.csv"
Rows Read: 460949, Total Rows Processed: 460949, Total
Chunk Time: 1.194 seconds
```

There's more...

The `rxImport()` function from `RevoScaleR` creates the XDF file and stores metadata for each column. The important thing is that the newly created `xdfFile` object is not in the R session's memory; rather the object just points to the location of the file in the persistent storage. You can call the file and perform further processing tasks. For example, if you want to see the variable's information, then `rxGetInfo()` will be useful. Here is some example code for seeing the variable's information:

```
rxGetInfo(xdfFile, getVarInfo = TRUE)

File name: D:\AllSync\Drive\Book-3\codeBundle\ch9\USAirlines2016.xdf
Number of observations: 5562425
Number of variables: 9
Number of blocks: 12
Compression type: zlib
Variable information:
Var 1: YEAR, Type: integer, Low/High: (2016, 2016)
Var 2: QUARTER, Type: integer, Low/High: (1, 4)
Var 3: MONTH, Type: integer, Low/High: (1, 12)
Var 4: DAY_OF_MONTH, Type: integer, Low/High: (1, 31)
Var 5: DAY_OF_WEEK, Type: integer, Low/High: (1, 7)
Var 6: ORIGIN, Type: character
Var 7: DEST, Type: character
Var 8: DEP_DELAY, Type: integer, Low/High: (-204, 2149)
Var 9: ARR_DELAY, Type: integer, Low/High: (-152, 2142)
```

So, this is how you can process a larger dataset without even importing it into R memory, and eventually you will achieve greater speed.

See also

There are other related functions that you can explore, such as `rxDataStep()`, `RxXdfData()`, and `rxTransform()` from the `RevoScaleR` library.

Processing data as a chunk

The XDF file allows for processing tasks more easily by applying the operation chunk by chunk. You do not need to import the entire dataset into the memory to do the processing tasks. To speed up the algorithm or any processing task, the chunk by chunk operation is quite helpful. In this recipe, you will see the chunk by chunk operation.

Getting ready

The XDF file you have created in the previous recipe *Creating an XDF file from CSV input* in this chapter, contains the following nine variables:

- YEAR
- QUARTER
- MONTH
- DAY_OF_MONTH
- DAY_OF_WEEK
- ORIGIN
- DEST
- DEP_DELAY
- ARR_DELAY

The objective of this recipe is to create a new binary variable binDelay, representing an indicator variable; if the departure delay is positive, then this new variable will get a value of 1, and 0 otherwise. Since you are going to use the XDF file for this operation, the task will be automatically split into chunks. You will need to load the RevoScaleR library for this operation.

How to do it...

The following are the steps for this recipe:

1. Create an object containing the filename and the location of the XDF file.
2. Load the RevoScaleR library.
3. Parse the XDF file through the rxDataSetp() function and perform the transformation.

Here's the R code corresponding to the preceding steps:

```
xdfFile <- file.path(getwd(), "USAirlines2016.xdf")
            rxDataStep(inData = xdfFile,
            outFile = xdfFile,
            transforms = list(binDelay = ifelse(DEP_DELAY>0,1,0)),
            overwrite = TRUE)
```

How it works...

You already know that you do not need to import the entire dataset into R memory, rather you will need to create a connection with the file. So, in the first step, you are creating the connection with the XDF file and the R session.

Later on, the `rxDataStep()` function takes the XDF filename with the location as input through the `inData` argument. If you want to create the new variable into the same XDF file, then the `outFile` argument will be of the same filename as `inData`; make sure that you have activated `overwrite = TRUE`.

Once you specify the `inData` and `outFile` arguments, the next and obvious thing is the definition of the transformation that you want to perform. In this case, your objective is to transform a `DEP_DELAY` variable into another new binary variable with `if DEP_DELAY>0`, then the new variable will get a value of `1`, or otherwise will get a value of `0`.

You should specify the transformation definition through the `transforms` argument. This is a named list containing the transformations. In this example, the new variable name is `binDelay`, and it has been created through the following code line:

```
transforms = list(binDelay = ifelse(DEP_DELAY>0,1,0))
```

Once you run the entire code block, it will show the following default progress output in the R console:

```
Rows Read: 445827, Total Rows Processed: 445827, Total Chunk Time:
0.946 seconds
Rows Read: 423889, Total Rows Processed: 869716, Total Chunk Time:
0.826 seconds
Rows Read: 423889, Total Rows Processed: 1293605, Total Chunk Time:
0.789 seconds
Rows Read: 461630, Total Rows Processed: 1755235, Total Chunk Time:
0.855 seconds
Rows Read: 479358, Total Rows Processed: 2234593, Total Chunk Time:
0.893 seconds
Rows Read: 487637, Total Rows Processed: 2722230, Total Chunk Time:
```

```
0.811 seconds
Rows Read: 502457, Total Rows Processed: 3224687, Total Chunk Time:
0.936 seconds
Rows Read: 498347, Total Rows Processed: 3723034, Total Chunk Time:
0.811 seconds
Rows Read: 454878, Total Rows Processed: 4177912, Total Chunk Time:
0.861 seconds
Rows Read: 472626, Total Rows Processed: 4650538, Total Chunk Time:
0.748 seconds
Rows Read: 450938, Total Rows Processed: 5101476, Total Chunk Time:
0.827 seconds
Rows Read: 460949, Total Rows Processed: 5562425, Total Chunk Time:
0.752 seconds
```

The processing time is dependent on the configuration of the computer that has been used for this task. So, you might get slightly different results.

If you want to print the first few rows of the data, then run the following line:

```
rxGetInfo(xdfFile, numRows = 5)
```

The preceding code line will give you the following output:

```
File name:
D:\AllSync\Drive\Book-3\codeBundle\ch9\USAirlines2016.xdf
   Number of observations: 5562425
   Number of variables: 10
   Number of blocks: 12
   Compression type: zlib
   Data (5 rows starting with row 1):
     YEAR QUARTER MONTH DAY_OF_MONTH DAY_OF_WEEK ORIGIN DEST DEP_DELAY
   1 2016       1     1            1           5    DTW  LAX         0
   2 2016       1     1            1           5    ATL  GRR         5
   3 2016       1     1            1           5    LAX  ATL         1
   4 2016       1     1            1           5    SLC  ATL         4
   5 2016       1     1            1           5    BZN  MSP        72


   ARR_DELAY   binDelay

         -24      FALSE
          -2       TRUE
         -13       TRUE
         -16       TRUE
         124       TRUE
```

There's more...

The `rxDataStep()` function is the most convenient function for data pre-processing. In this example, you have done a very simple transformation. There are other very useful options within this function, which are as follows:

- `transformFunc`: If you want to use an external function where you have defined all of your required transformation, this argument will give you that opportunity. Using this option, you can perform any complex operation as required.
- `transformVars`: This argument will give you an easy way to specify variables that are required within `transformFunc` or the `transforms` argument.
- `transformPackages`: Sometimes you might have used specialized functions from other libraries for the transformation task. You can explicitly specify the name of that library within `rxDataStep()` so that you do not need to load the library beforehand. It will automatically call the necessary libraries and complete the task on the fly.

See also

There are various other related functions to consider. Specifically, you are advised to consider the following functions from the `RevoScaleR` library:

- `rxImport()`
- `RxXdfData()`
- `rxTransform()`

Comparing computation time with data frame and XDF

Computation time is one of the important things to consider while doing big data analytics. The efficiency of the algorithm is assessed by the computation time along with other parameters. The objective of using an XDF file instead of the default R data frame is to achieve high speed computation. In this recipe, you will compare the performance in terms of computation time using the default data frame and the XDF file.

Getting ready

Suppose you have a dataset stored in two different formats. The first one is an CSV file containing nine variables, and the other one is the XDF file containing the same variables. The following are the variable names:

- YEAR
- QUARTER
- MONTH
- DAY_OF_MONTH
- DAY_OF_WEEK
- ORIGIN
- DEST
- DEP_DELAY
- ARR_DELAY

The objective is to calculate mean departure delay for each combination of origin and destination airports. The required library for this recipe is RevoScaleR.

How to do it...

The following are the steps to calculate the processing time to find out mean departure delay for each combination of origin and destination airports:

1. Set up a working directory where the CSV and XDF files are stored.
2. Read the CSV file.
3. Calculate the mean departure delay for each combination of origin and destination airport and report the processing time.
4. Create an object connecting the XDF file with the R session.
5. Load the RevoScaleR library.
6. Calculate the mean departure delay for each combination of the origin and destination airport and report the processing time.

The following shows the implementation of the preceding steps:

```
# Step-1
setwd("D:/AllSync/Drive/Book-3/codeBundle/ch9")

# Step-2
system.time(
  usairlineCSV <- read.csv("csv_USAairlines2016.csv")
)

# Step-3
system.time(
meanDelay<- with(usairlineCSV, aggregate(DEP_DELAY,
by=list(ORIGIN, DEST), FUN= "mean", na.rm=T))
  )

# Step-4
system.time(
  xdfFile <- file.path(getwd(), "USAirlines2016.xdf")
)

# Step-5
system.time(
  sumstatxdf <- rxSummary(DEP_DELAY~ORIGIN:DEST,
  summaryStats = "Mean", data = xdfFile)
)
```

How it works...

In the *step 1* from the previous section, the directory location where the CSV file and the XDF file are stored is located. Then in *step 2*, the read.csv() function imports the entire dataset into an R session for further processing. In *step 3*, using the aggregate function, the mean departure delay is calculated, and in the same step, the processing time is calculated using the system.time() function.

The processing time for each section is as follows:

```
> system.time(
+   usairlineCSV <- read.csv("csv_USAairlines2016.csv")
+ )
  user  system elapsed
 19.11    0.51   19.72
```

It took almost 20 seconds to read the entire CSV file into R memory. Here is the time requirement for calculating the mean:

```
> system.time(
+   meanDelay<- with(usairlineCSV, aggregate(DEP_DELAY,
      by=list(ORIGIN, DEST), FUN= "mean", na.rm=T))
+ )

   user  system elapsed
   7.02    0.34    7.37
```

It took more than 7 seconds to calculate the mean delay for each combination of the origin and destination airports.

In *step 4*, the xdfFile object creates a connection between the actual XDF file and the R session. Later on, in *step 5*, this object is used as the input data, and then the mean departure delay is calculated. The required time for *step 4* and *step 5* is given as follows:

```
> system.time(
+   xdfFile <- file.path(getwd(), "USAirlines2016.xdf")
+ )

   user  system elapsed
      0       0       0

> system.time(
+   sumstatxdf <- rxSummary(DEP_DELAY~ORIGIN:DEST,
      summaryStats = "Mean", data = xdfFile)
+ )

Rows Read: 5562425, Total Rows Processed: 5562425, Total Chunk
Time: 0.335 seconds
Computation time: 0.477 seconds.
   user  system elapsed
   1.21    0.00    1.83
```

Creating a connection with an XDF file took less than 1 second, and calculating the mean for each combination of origin and destination only took less than 2 seconds.

There's more…

The example implemented in this recipe is the simplest example showing the difference in computation time when you use the default R data frame and an XDF file. You can perform more complex operations at high speed using an XDF file. You can use a remote cluster computing facility to boost the computation speed.

Linear regression with larger data (rxFastLiner)

Linear regression is one of the most popular algorithms to predict the numeric outcome based on observed features. The default implementation in R for the linear regression is the lm() function. For a larger dataset with a large number of variables, this could take a very long time to run. The rxFastLinear() function for the RevoScaleR library offers a very fast implementation of linear regression with a larger dataset with many variables. In this recipe, you will build a linear regression model to predict arrival delay time as a function of the origin and destination airport along with the departure delay and the day of the week.

Getting ready

To build a linear regression model to predict the arrival delay time, you will need to have the RevoScaleR library. The dataset for this recipe will be the XDF file containing the following variables:

- YEAR
- QUARTER
- MONTH
- DAY_OF_MONTH
- DAY_OF_WEEK
- ORIGIN
- DEST
- DEP_DELAY
- ARR_DELAY

The objective is to build a linear regression model with ARR_DELAY as the dependant (outcome variable) and ORIGIN, DEST, DEP_DELAY, and DAY_OF_WEEK as the features (independent variables). Note that the variables ORIGIN and DEST will be treated as factor (categorical) variables.

How to do it...

The steps to building a linear regression model using the rxFastLinear() function from the RevoScaleR library are as follows:

1. Connect the XDF file with the R session by creating an object in R.
2. Load the RevoScaleR library.
3. Specify the outcome and feature columns into the formula and parse through the rxFastLinear() function.

   Here's the exact R code to implement the preceding steps:

   ```
   setwd("D:/AllSync/Drive/Book-3/codeBundle/ch9")
   xdfFile <- file.path(getwd(), "USAirlines2016.xdf")
   linMod <- rxFastLinear(ARR_DELAY~DEP_DELAY+ORIGIN+DEST+DAY_OF_WEEK,
   type = "regression", data = xdfFile)
   ```

How it works...

The implementation is very simple and easy to understand. The rxFastLinear() function is capable of implementing a classification model and regression model. In this example, the code is for a linear regression model. Usually, the type is determined by the type of the outcome variable, but it is always good to specify the type of model using the type argument.

The function takes a model formula as an input and the data source. All other arguments were evaluated at their default values. Since there were two factor variables, the ultimate model contains a lot more variables than the variable specified in the model formula. Each of the values of the ORIGIN and DEST variables is represented by a binary variable. The following is the default console output after a complete execution of the function:

```
Automatically adding a MinMax normalization transform,
use 'norm=Warn' or 'norm=No' to turn this behavior off.
Beginning read for block: 1
Rows Read: 5562425, Read Time: 0.36, Transform Time: 0
Beginning read for block: 2
```

```
No rows remaining. Finished reading data set.
Beginning read for block: 1
Rows Read: 5562425, Read Time: 0.291, Transform Time: 0
Beginning read for block: 2
Beginning read for block: 1
Rows Read: 5562425, Read Time: 0.295, Transform Time: 0
Beginning read for block: 2
No rows remaining. Finished reading data set.
Using 2 threads to train.
Automatically choosing a check frequency of 2.
Warning: Skipped 81469 instances with missing features/label
during training
Auto-tuning parameters: maxIterations = 2.
Auto-tuning parameters: L2 = 1E-06.
Auto-tuning parameters: L1Threshold (L1/L2) = 0.25.
Using model from last iteration.
Not training a calibrator because it is not needed.
Elapsed time: 00:00:14.6034061
Elapsed time: 00:00:00.1922793
```

Once the model is built, you can perform a prediction and extract other information as required.

There's more...

The preceding example contains the simplest way of building a linear regression model using the rxFastLinear() function. If your dataset is large enough to fit into a single computer's memory, then you can run this model in a remote cluster computing node. To run this model in a remote cluster computing node, you need to create a computing context using RxComputeContext(). Also, you can pass the computing context through the computeContext argument.

To get a predicted outcome, you could use the rxPredict() function along with the new dataset.

See also

There are other Machine Learning algorithms implemented within the RevoScaleR and MicrosoftML libraries. You are advised to look into the documentation of the MicrosoftML and RevoScaleR libraries for other models.

Index